Overcoming the Devastation of

Legal Abuse Syndrome

Beyond Rage

Karin P. Huffer M.S., M.F.T.

PUBLISHED BY FULKORT PRESS

Discounts on quantity orders for non-profit and
educational organizations available.
To order, call:
(800) 829-8969
Compuserve - 74537,546
America On Line - fulkort@aol.com

The lawsuit portrayed on the cover of this book and
the names contained herein have been changed to protect
the privacy of the individuals mentioned.
No legal advice is given in this book.

Library of Congress Pre-Assigned Number
94-066672

Huffer, Karin P.
   Legal Abuse Syndrome / Karin P. Huffer M.S., M.F.T. — 1st ed.

ISBN 0-9641786-0-5

© 1995 by Karin P. Huffer
All Rights Reserved.
Printed in the United States of America
First Printing, June 1995

Contents

Acknowledgements i

Preface iii

Introduction xii

1. Invisible Hostages 1
2. The Epidemic 19

Eight Steps to Recovery

3. Debriefing 29
4. Grieving 51
5. Obsession 69
6. Blaming 83
7. Deshaming 107

Contents

8.	Reframing	131
9.	Empowerment	153
10.	Recovery	193

Conclusion 213

Epilogue 217

Bibliography 221

Glossary 229

Appendix A - Clinical Post Traumatic Stress Disorder Defined

Appendix B - Resources for the Empowerment of the Ordinary Person

Appendix C - Victims - Witness Protection Act 1982. Representative Jack Brooks Press Release

Appendix D - Worksheets

Dedication

To all lawyers, judges, and bureaucrats who do not abuse their positions, who care with sensitivity about those they serve, and who serve with courage regardless of budget, overcrowding, or intimidation. To the Legal Abuse Syndrome victims who trusted me, shared and have inspired this work.

Acknowledgments

Each person listed below gave to this endeavor and to me in a most meaningful way. Without the support, involvement, input, and intelligence of the following people, *Legal Abuse Syndrome/Beyond Rage* could have not been fully germinated, defined, and put forth in this book.

Jonna Stephenson patiently listened, defined, critiqued and was there year after year.

Heidi Horton Stephenson edited and reacted with profound encouragement early on.

Chuck Milden's help was indispensable, Chuck turned my manuscript into a real book by designing its eye catching cover, page layout and artwork. Then he typeset the entire book.

Tom Read shared his personal experiences and mastery of the law, and responded like a rudder when asked for help.

Claire Quigley gave generously from her soul, continually inspiring expanded ideas such as the "Invisible Target."

Billie Gremain gave the most generous gift known to man. She sat by my side reacting, editing, looking up tedious grammatical details, and gave to me and this project her time and herself.

Julie Murphy, Dan Geiger and Vickie Moehrle for proofreading and offering their continual encouragement.

J.D., Jason, and Jordan, my family, who ran errands, cooked, and were available for the mundane to release me to do this work.

John Johnston, Claudia A. Munoz-Jackson, Nancy Clark who pioneered the seminar and affirmed the validity of this theory.

Connie Oglesby helped me organize the mounds of research and rough copies, and gave generously of her time and encouragement.

Barbara Kelly became a friend, and expanded to new horizons the dimensions and direction of this work.

Bill Connolly, Lloyd Hardy, Mike Kilbourn, Dale Robertson, and all Victims for their encouragement and feedback.

Laura Herlovich opened her knowledge and resources to the promotion of this project.

Al Adask freely gave publication suggestions and encouragement and remains supportive of this endeavor.

Daryl Williams, Esq., a lawyer, who said, "This book is critically important for all of society as well as victims and lawyers."

Bruce Yarborough, a sensitive and caring FBI agent whose suggestions validated and balanced.

Mr. & Mrs. Dick Pickens for devoting themselves to the betterment of the judicial system.

Corky Strandburg for being an inspiring pillar in my life.

And finally, to all my anonymous patients who trusted me and helped me to see the theory.

Preface

- If you are deeply disillusioned and feeling oppressed as an American citizen, resulting from experience with our justice system, you may be suffering from Legal Abuse Syndrome.

- If you've been a litigant in court and justice was not to be obtained at any price, you may be suffering from Legal Abuse Syndrome.

- If you fantasize about an act of vigilante vengeance because it seems like the only recourse, you may be suffering from Legal Abuse Syndrome.

- If you've reported a crime and found that you were punished instead of the criminal, you may be suffering from Legal Abuse Syndrome.

Preface

- If creativity and dreams have been left in the past because their development was ripped from you and torn to shreds by your protective systems, you may be suffering from Legal Abuse Syndrome.

- If you feel numb, disconnected, and vulnerable, you may be suffering from Legal Abuse Syndrome.

- If you feel that the "system" will defeat you at every turn and there is nothing you can do about it, you may be suffering from Legal Abuse Syndrome.

- If you feel that you have been victimized twice, once by a perpetrator and then by your protective system, you may be suffering from Legal Abuse Syndrome.

- If you feel that you are a decent and honorable taxpayer who's been subjected to "cruel and unusual punishment" by lawyers, judges, and officers of the court, you may be suffering from Legal Abuse Syndrome.

Some will deny that Legal Abuse Syndrome (LAS) exists. They will remind us that we have an adversarial system of justice. Abusers will be written off as adversaries battling for their clients. Victims will be nothing more than casualties of a "fight for justice." Others will worry that victims of LAS will want compensation for their psychological injuries. Skeptics will ask, "Aren't LAS victims just malingerers wanting more from the system?"

Legal Abuse Syndrome

I do not indict the legal profession, fine judges, and hard working public servants. I applaud those who serve their clients well in any milieu. We do not bash any organization or profession in this book. Lawyers, judges, FBI agents, police officers and investigators have all crossed my private practice and helped me to delineate the abuse of power that permeates every profession. Many of these professionals are themselves invisible victims and need the support of the public.

Abusers are studied in this book as a method of exposing to LAS victims the predicament that oppresses them. The systems are explored in the light of victims' experiences. The psycholegal condition is revealed along with skills to help the victim cope with abusers of his systems. The scope is a large one for a marriage and family therapist or fellow victim to tackle. It may feel unwieldy and threatening to the reader. However, reading and rereading has produced results and has motivated me to risk a big project, and perhaps an unpopular one, in behalf of those invisible victims who can heal in spite of systems without a cure.

A firm warning to those who would use the following material to damage or discredit any citizen in any manner:

> **LEGAL ABUSE SYNDROME IS A NATURAL AND NORMAL RESPONSE TO AN ABNORMAL, UNNATURAL, CUMULATIVE TRAUMA, AS WITH ALL POST TRAUMATIC STRESS DISORDERS. ANY ATTEMPT BY ANY PERSON TO DISCREDIT AN INDIVIDUAL'S TESTIMONY, CHARACTER, OR ACTIONS DUE TO THEIR SUFFERING FROM LAS IS TO CLEARLY DEMONSTRATE THE ABERRANT**

Preface

NATURE OF OUR SYSTEM OF PROBLEM-SOLVING. ANY ALLY OF CIVILIZATION MUST CLEARLY IDENTIFY SUCH BEHAVIOR AS ABUSIVE, PUT A HALT TO DESTRUCTIVE ACTIONS, AND DEVOTE THEIR ENERGIES TO RESTORATION OF VICTIMS OF THE "SYSTEM."

No one likes to think of himself as a victim. Immediately, it conjures an image of a loser or someone making poor life-choices. Yet in spite of resistance to facing our victimization, legal abuses have become common. When abuses occur, victims are created. We either have to face that we are victimized or accept an aberration to civilized living as being "just the way it is."

Laws provide for courts, agencies, law enforcement bureaucracies, and regulatory services. We depend on them to resolve our disputes and to protect our cherished rights. When they fail, our nation must deal with the victims and vigilantes left in the wake of officially sanctioned wrongdoing.

In this book, we will explore cases that are shocking and fascinating. They illustrate abuses perpetrated by our legally instituted protective systems and the pain and suffering that results. Citizens are driven "Beyond Rage." However startling and moving our cases may be, we have only touched a segment of their lives and experiences. Each case has, left unrevealed, depth of trauma and complication that would be prohibitive in space and time to write about in one book.

This work results from my experiences of the past twenty years as a marriage and family therapist in private practice. Throughout my career, a certain discomfort gnawed at me regarding clients who attended my various groups and seminars. While the seminars dealt with the subjects of codependency, substance abuse, parenting, divorce adjustment, assertiveness, stress, or whatever the current topic dictated, there always remained the walking wounded. Those were clients whose true source of pain was not recognized by family or friends. Worse, it was never clearly defined by helping professionals. With no diagnosis, their condition could not be targeted for treatment. Invisible trauma nebulously danced around the topics, never to be healed in these hungry participants.

It wasn't until a white-collar crime was perpetrated on my family that I saw these walking wounded with uncomfortably opened eyes. After nearly a decade of struggling with the justice system, and working with other such victims, I have concluded that the enormous betrayals and inefficiencies that make up bureaucratic post-crime experiences are literally attacking the emotional health of this nation. Victims have no satisfying place to turn. Rage accumulates and its sequelae have reached epidemic proportions.

A therapist must, of course, check such observations against the danger of inaccurately projecting onto a client personal feelings or attitudes that go beyond therapeutic use of self. I have done that. Even more uncomfortably now, I see the massive validation of my theory by participants in the "Beyond Rage" seminars. Still theoretical, but deadly serious, is the thesis of this book that victims in America are, first, assaulted by crime and, secondly, by abuses of power and authority administered by the systems their tax dollars support to provide due process of law. In short, they get a "double whammy."

People of principle find their decency, trustworthiness, responsibility, and use of their courts trounced by systems that perpetrate

Preface

judicial and bureaucratic atrocities. Americans who follow a code of conscience encounter a profound imbalance between the abuses of power perpetrated by those entrusted with the systems and the prohibitive conscience of the ordinary person to violation of values and laws. At the heart of this book is the threatened psychic underpinning of the American citizen which is tied into the Constitutionally protected rights that we depend upon. To imperil the basic freedoms which Americans are taught are their birthright is to jeopardize conditions of trust and safety necessary for a healthy, productive life.

Victims challenge the finest of counseling techniques. The lack of closure combines with prolonged cruel and unusual punishment exerted by the court system. Ongoing strain of litigation then interfaces with psychological issues. Diagnoses are tricky and dynamic. Healing techniques and strategies are interrupted by the trauma of the proceedings or behaviors of court personnel. Stress reduction training is of marginal value for a litigant who will regularly be administered another dose of outrage. The best of family intervention is defeated if the family court renders a visitation arrangement that destroys continuity in the raising of the children, or if the current custodial parent is harassed and stalked, unprotected by the law enforcement system.

Outrage is tough enough. Beyond rage is terribly painful territory. I caution the reader that to earnestly use this self-help material for healing purposes will be challenging. On the other hand, if you choose to stay beyond rage, you exist in a type of living death. So victims of the systems are caught between a tough place and a really hard place. Go slowly, get involved in groups, if possible, but don't let your lifeblood be stripped from you without a fight. This book

Legal Abuse Syndrome

will help to get you back on your fighting feet. You won't change massive systems or reform your country in all likelihood. However, when all of the trauma has been processed, you will become an empowered, effective individual again.

More and more, helping professionals are being confronted by "psycholegal" issues. Patients are driven beyond rage over an extended period of time, during which victims travel an isolated road. The impact of the invisible assaults usually are ignored.

Vigilante violence results when the needs of the majority are not being met by the systems (Tucker). What of the gentle and decent person who values a law abiding mode of life? Unless the unique needs of these victims are identified and healing processes made accessible to them, the cost in pain, suffering, disillusionment, and shutdown of creativity to the individual and society is immeasurable.

Karin Pearson Huffer

Foreword

As the former United States Trustee for Region 17, covering bankruptcy administration for the Northern and Eastern districts of California and the district of Nevada, my perspective is that of one with first hand experience with the "realities" of the bankruptcy system.

The United States bankruptcy system was intended to be the most advanced, compassionate and humane system anywhere in the civilized western world. Unfortunately, especially in the area of Chapter 11 bankruptcy, the system has often resulted in creating greater pain.

Competent, confident outgoing entrepreneurs are reduced to "Shell-shocked" paranoia, unable to make the most basic decisions. Polite, law-abiding individuals are transformed into raging extremists, after being lulled unsuspectingly in many cases into believing that they will emerge from bankruptcy able to pick up the pieces with a fresh start.

Karin Huffer's book, in my opinion, is a most timely and worthy effort to explain the trauma and pain suffered by those who have been victimized by legal abuse.

Anthony G. Sousa, Esq.

Introduction

Legal Abuse Syndrome is a book which helps victims overcome the pain caused by their psychological reaction to profound and prolonged injustice. Those who seek justice have been victimized by either deception or violence. When a victim pursues justice he becomes engaged in a "shotgun wedding" of sorts which unites the psychological and legal issues into a psycholegal condition. Recovery requires both psychological attention and legal closure. T h e condition, which I have named "Legal Abuse Syndrome" (LAS), is a chronic "psycholegal" Post Traumatic Stress Disorder which complicates the victim's ability to adequately defend himself or herself against further assaults or to effectively fight for rights, at a moment when victims most need their creative powers. LAS is the obscure factor that is exploited by unscrupulous attorneys, white-collar criminals, and abusers of authority.

We will meet victims who suffer from LAS. Each story vividly portrays the struggle for freedom against systems that fail their proprietors, the taxpayers. The stories are of real people put to the test of character; bravery takes on a quiet dimension. I resist the term "common people" because it alludes to sameness. These are unique

Introduction

and talented individuals whose common thread lies only in their traumas. "Ordinary" is a more appropriate adjective in that they are unknown, private performers and reflective of the majority of Americans.

James was an ordinary man with a dream. He put hard work behind the dream and brought it to near completion. A big bank and a contractor conspired and together used the bankruptcy system to take the product of twenty years of James' life.

Judy was a trusting mother and real estate salesperson. She met a man and married him. She found that the identity of the man she married was falsified. He had been three separate people in his life. Three complete sets of false identities had seen this man through feigned lives across the nation.

John was ready for retirement. A trusted employee and an attorney conspired to take his company. John is fighting for his financial life at an age that was planned for comfortable retirement. His wife worries that the stress and trauma will kill him.

Tom suffered financial collapse as a result of improper actions of a judge who would not enforce a jury's decision. Tom took on his own legal battle. He has fought for nearly a decade in court. His appreciation of the Constitutional plan for American justice has grown along with his determination to protect it.

P.J. was ripped-off by a family member. The con placed her in conflict between the family members and standing up for herself against the con artist. The amount of money isn't huge. Her pain has been profound.

Chloe was rejected, divorced, and assumed to be a woman who could not put up a fight in court to protect her share of the estate. Chloe set a new standard for perseverance and creativity in her court battles. Her prominent husband, with his power-oriented ways, is left in shock as Chloe begins to turn her case around. The reader will be shocked as well.

Manny followed family tradition and stood up for himself against the odds. Manny allowed his emotions to dominate his case.

Each of these victims suffers from LAS. They would not have developed the condition if the institutions that are paid to regulate and protect the citizens had functioned ethically and competently. Massive system failures greeted each of them. Their experiences and those of others will guide us from their points of victimization through the eight steps toward recovery.

Psycholegal LAS victims have exceeded rage in the human emotional experience. This book is the helping manual for these walking wounded who suffer from the cumulative effects of a criminal or deceptive assault followed by further trauma from experiences with the justice system, professionals, and/or bureaucracies. *Legal Abuse Syndrome* exposes a completely preventable condition. LAS takes the victim "Beyond Rage." This book brings the victim back from the implosive, devastating cycle of LAS. Eight steps provide the road map and survival course that guides the victim from the points of impact of the assaults through the brutalities of the systems too often encountered during the aftermath of crime.

Introduction

Chapter 1

Invisible Hostages
The kidnapping of the soul

"I do not feel free or able to pursue happiness in my country."
Ken, LAS Victim and American citizen

Invisible Crimes - The Dilemma

Victims are created in two ways: by violence or by deceit. Either type of assault immediately renders the victim hostage to the perpetrator(s). Victims feel as helpless as small children. Personal control becomes the issue. Adult autonomy is formed by a perception of trust. Psychologist Erik H. Erikson calls this feeling "basic trust." The child must sense this degree of invulnerability in order to grow. The long, hard battle to adulthood is accomplished when one has the ability to take charge of one's own life (Bard). The belief that the world is manageable allows a sense of psychological balance. A deceptive crime instantly takes the victim into a hostage relationship. It is like a kidnapping of the soul. Equilibrium is lost. Regardless of the individual's ability to accommodate stress, all victims must work out of a hostage relationship with the offender.

Violent crime dominates the headlines and consumes most of the moneys that are allocated for victim assistance, yet white-collar crimes are rising faster than violent crime (Kropatkin & Kusic). It is naive to believe that victims emerge from these assaults unscathed.

All professionals who respond to the crimes-lawyers, judges, police officers, IRS agents (who always show up at the end of the ordeal), the media, and health professionals-bear responsibility for the protection of the victims' mental and emotional health in the aftermath of crime. (The worst serial killer receives millions of dollars to protect his rights, his health, and his well-being.) The victim is just beginning to gain recognition of his needs. Still, survivors and victims too often fade into a neglected judicial oblivion. Unlike violent crime, deceptive assaults quietly wound that very sacred, inner place which is the essence of self. (Shown in Figure 1 are examples of invisible crimes and betrayals). Although the attack is invisible, it is as brutal as violent assault. Profound changes take place in the victim's life, yet they can go completely unnoticed. The victim becomes isolated. He or she may rise every day, go to work, come home, appear at family functions, and look relatively normal; however, it is as if layers of cellophane wrap have enveloped him in a numb cocoon.

Symptoms of Hostage Stage

- Intrusive thoughts and nightmares seep in through the numbness.

- There is difficulty concentrating.

- Memories are painful; flashbacks are unrelenting.

- The victims will route themselves around reminders, and cringe from people, songs, news stories, or events that trigger memories and intense distress.

- Ordinary activities require tremendous energy; the victim is mentally, emotionally, and physically exhausted.

- The victim now trusts no one.

- Not trusting has reached the point that it has begun to erode the quality of the victim's life.

- He or she feels off-balance.

- Creativity is blunted.

- Intensity of interest in the world around the victim is dulled.

- Tension/ anxiety/ depression cycle sets in; the victim may self-medicate with alcohol or drugs.

- Fear is the main motivator of life's decisions. The victim becomes hyperreactive, hypervigilant, and obsessive.

- Physical changes take place as stressors continue to pound away at those victims who try to stand up for themselves.

- 85% of victims will manifest physical symptoms. There is significant evidence that fat in the diet, cigarette smoking, salt and lack of exercise have much less to do with coronary heart disease and other stress-related

Invisible Crimes and Victimization from Betrayals of Trust

- White Collar Crime
- Credit Card Scams
- Savings & Loan Scandals
- S.L.A.P.P Suits
- Misrepresentation
- Electronic/Computer Scams
- Extortion of Rights/ Cash Violence
- Insider Trading
- Embezzlement
- Theft of an Idea/ Creative Effort
- Fraud
- Commissionectomies
- Slander
- Libel
- Consumers Rip-offs
- Racketeering
- Insurance Rip-offs
- Betrayals of Trust
- Pollution of Rationality, Lies, Lies, Lies...
- Bureaucracy Abuses
- Conflict of Interest
- Strategic Abuse of Process
- Oppressive Corporate Behavior
- Breach of Fiduciary Duty
- Bankruptcy Fraud
- Bribery
- Cronyism
- Business Bullying
- Political Scams
- No Faith
- Family Crimes
- Divorce and Family Court Abuses
- Contempt of Court/ Child Support
- IRS Abuses
- No Fair Dealing
- Malpractice
- Insurance Fraud
- Perjury
- Forgery
- Environmental Assault/Toxins
- Con Artists
- Harassment
- False Advertising
- Sexual Harassment
- Crimes of the Heart
- Credit Bashing
- Bait and Switch
- Counterfeiting
- Blackmail
- Obscene Phone Calls
- Breach of Contract

Figure 1 - Invisible Crimes

illnesses than do rage, anger, and frustration. (McQuade)

When a Hostage Seeks Justice

Jeopardy becomes the theme of the victim's lifestyle when he/she then acts as a witness or litigant. The assault may be only a traumatic first step in a protracted legal process. Typically, the victim remains an emotional hostage for many years. Not only does the justice system move slowly, delays are used as strategy by attorneys to weaken their opposition economically and emotionally. Delays will cause further losses in the victim's life as pressure is sustained on family life, work life, physical health, and the bank account. All facets of the victim's life are at risk and under attack during litigation.

Helplessness in the face of jeopardy is the formula for Post Traumatic Stress Disorder. The citizen is never more jeopardized or helpless than when his entire protective system is clearly functioning as a selfish taker instead of a protector. How did majority opinion and need become disarmed within our justice system?

An Evolution of Institutionalized Abuse of Power

The moral core which forms the foundation of American values is the lifeblood that sustains the victim's hope. Decency, our most cherished and delicate human resource, hangs in the balance of the scales of justice. If the system exists for protection of the citizen and is supported by tax dollars, it is assumed to represent common decency. Other than a few rascals, we expect to encounter professionals who sanction goodness as we persevere through the courts.

It is against this backdrop that judges, attorneys, regulators, and others, who elect to be solely self-serving, find their prey. Attorneys are reported to knowingly exhaust their client's resources and leave their clients vulnerable. They make "deals" to preserve their political status with their colleagues. Judges will find for the more rich and powerful in spite of evidence. These are the pathologic elements that further betray victims. In such cases, judges, lawyers and others entrusted with the justice system become host-toxic parasites. They draw on courts but do not protect the system, rendering the courts non-functional for the purpose that it was created. Therefore the court is simply not there to help people resolve disputes, punish offenders of the law, and protect the citizens. (Marston, Dershowitz).

Keen tells us that in the 1800's, a man's character was comprised of citizenship, duty, democracy, work, building, golden deeds, outdoor life, conquest, honor, reputation, morals, manners, and integrity. He lived for the good of the community. Then came the industrial revolution, and the "self" has emerged beyond the community.

Warring entered the boardroom. Corporate giants, nonhuman entities who answer to stockholders based upon bottom line figures, go to court against individuals. The hearing is expected to be fair and provide equality. It is the duty of the judge to provide such a forum.

XYZ Corporation versus private citizen, John Brown, is nearly impossible to equalize. John is fortunate if he can afford one attorney. XYZ will send a team. Every document costs John significant dollars. XYZ's team is on salary. John may have never contributed to a judge's campaign. XYZ contributes to all judges' campaigns. John cares about the system, his children, justice, and himself. XYZ's attorneys are out to be heroes for the corporation's bottom - line benefit at any price. Corporations were not created with a conscience or concern for the mental health of the nation. Serving of self has become paramount. These emotional hostages ask, "Do attorneys intend to destroy their country and to render all decent citizens mentally ill?" "Is it fair for the IRS to attack a citizen and hold him responsible for a business transaction simply because he is the only one they can locate?" "Are the courts only toys for the wealthy and tools by which the wealthy fleece the population?" or, "Are we experiencing a second, invisible economic holocaust perpetrated on middle America and the poor?"

The methods used by the criminal and his defense attorney would sometimes cause us to believe that the above is true. Alfred Adask writes that he was not prepared for a full frontal attack when he went to court. He expected a hearing, not warfare. His case withered under the toxic formulas used by the attorneys. (Antishyster Appendix B):

Defy	-	Truth and procedure were defied
Deny	-	Facts and law were ignored
Delay	-	Time exceeded reason
Deplete	-	Expense exceeded reason
Destroy	-	Distortions replaced truth

Devastate - Money/beliefs/hope gone
Decay - System no longer useful to people

The disillusioned certainly have to wonder about the motives of those professionals who would lie, intimidate, and destroy as part of their "profession." Is it a warped rite of passage to economic manhood? Sam Keen, *Fire in the Belly*, writes, "Could it be that men are determined to be greedy, aggressive, and brutish? Does excess testosterone condemn us to violence and early heart attacks?" He is questioning maleness. Yet it is found that where females have entered the law and the boardroom, softer, gentler styles have not been the rule. Obviously, gender does not dictate abuses of power.

Rather than the intent to destroy the system as mentioned above, except for a few unsavory instances, the matter seems more one of an evolution. It is, however, a dangerous metamorphosis toward specialization in the abuse of power and sophisticated violence. The adversarial system supports lies, slander, distortion, and attack if it is in defense of a client. The acts are too destructive to ignore and too serious for victims to simply blame and complain about. Kensteen Olsen, founder of "Justice for All," believes that the adversarial system will one day be viewed as ridiculously as jousting is today as a means of resolving disputes.

Profile of a Hostage

Let's look at the story of James. James is a young man, who, after a deceptive crime, entered that judicial oblivion. James was in his forties. His dark eyes flashed with conviction as he told a story that was a quagmire of legal entanglement. He related it took him about 15 years to gain the properties that became the booty of this crime.

The Story of James
(As shared by James and his wife)

James had worked seven days a week, put in long hours, and continually challenged himself by tackling tougher levels of real estate from selling houses to sophisticated commercial aspects of the profession. He earned and saved with whole-hearted commitment. Finally, he negotiated and purchased, through long and arduous years of payments, three properties chosen to be his life's work. He had been a poor kid. This was proof of the American dream, something important to James. James was energized and joyous at that time.

The American dream was a major factor in James' survival. At his core he exudes the entrepreneurial spirit. He talked from his heart of artistic creativity and of hunger. It is hard to believe that he was born to abusive parents. Lots of kids were abused in the forties. It wasn't called abuse then. It was called being strict and no one interfered but, when his spirit and their oppressiveness collided, life's hope was at risk.

It helped that he did well in school. It was there that the promise was taught. The American dream reached into his life and helped him resist the punitive, crushing rigidity of home. "You may create your own destiny" he read in John Locke. Dream, reach out, and, thanks to brilliant men of 200 years ago, your life is in your hands.

The dream provided the faith and hope that allowed him to move away from his parents at sixteen, work a variety of jobs, all at the same time, and pursue an education at the University of Michigan. His ambitions were being satisfied, his neuroses and abuse-born shame soothed. He worked too hard, moved up the ladder, endured tremendous discomfort, and was a true, tired American living a dream. He tells that he hit the ground running every morning. After 20 years of such work, his net worth was $3,000,000. His credit was impeccable. He was a resident of his community for 23 years and was well respected. He had some business clout. It was time to implement the balance of his dream. The time was right to build on the three properties, manage them, and eventually sell them in order to educate the children and retire comfortably. Then, he would turn to artistic endeavors.

He shared a drawing of his first project. It reflected his aesthetic notions. It was a building that looked liked small buildings set together in a cozy pattern. There were variations in roof lines that were tasteful and drew the interest of a passerby. A sports lounge was placed beside a restaurant to generate immediate cash flow. It was obvious that careful study produced this first solo project.

James obtained a loan from a local bank to build the project and another loan, called a permanent loan, from an out-of-state lender who specialized in financing projects after completion and after tenants began lease payments. A major local bank approved the loan. All sacrifices were diminished by the excitement of this moment. Although the bare property looked like moonscape, this piece of desert was to blossom. Beautifully structured and landscaped, the property would provide services that responded to the market needs of the community.

James, being a responsible person, was happy to secure the loan with personal holdings because it was the first 7-figure loan he had made on his own and, of course, he vowed to be responsible to and for this project. He obtained expert legal advice and architectural work, and had selected a federally regulated bank. The bank, by contract, had the right to approve the contractor and the tenants. A licensed contractor was chosen and approved, and the project was begun.

The events that were to follow could have only been predicted by writers of cynical, sleazy, 'B' movies. A trap had been set by the bank. It is a saga of the corporate wringing out of staple values that hold a culture together. James' story is the documentary of thousands of Americans who are targeted by business and legal predators. These thousands of Americans are not stupid. They are not failures; however, they often feel like it.

James case-study will be told in the context of LAS, his trek beyond rage and the steps to recovery. His hope is to share in a way that will help to reframe the invisible victim from the image of shame, pain, and impotence. Victims can be society's "smart bombs" in helping to identify wrongdoing and prevent its propagation.

James and Legal Abuse Syndrome
Outrage explodes; beyond rage there is an implosion. Life's agenda turns inward into a survival cycle. Anger turns to rage; rage turns to outrage. If assaults through neglect or abuse continue, the victim becomes one of the "walking wounded" who are beyond rage (Figure 2, Path to LAS).

Briefly James' assaults moved in this manner:
1. The contractor refused to follow proper codes in constructing the building causing him to lose his license to build in the City. He behaved as if James was not in control. The contractor embezzled $400,000 by not paying costs on the job.
2. James formally requested that the bank cooperate with him in replacing the contractor. The bank refused.
3. James discovered that the banker and contractor had met privately; with no explanation, the banker had issued a cashiers check for $100,000 to the contractor out of James' loan.
4. James added a contractor to complete the suites for tenants so he could qualify for the permanent loan. This move would pay the construction loan

Legal Abuse Syndrome

Victim's actions and emotions interact with traumatic responses from protective systems. The path to Beyond Rage.

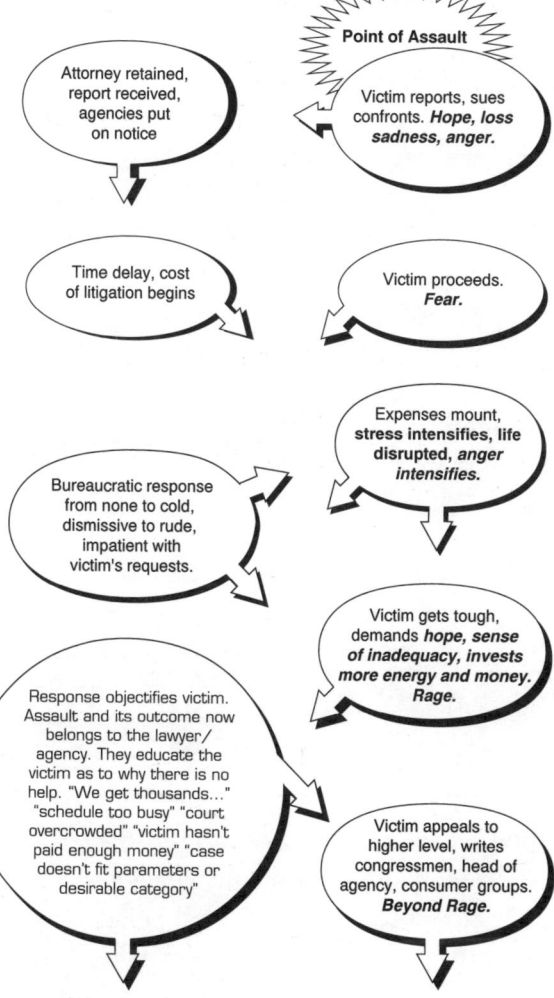

Figure 2 - Path to Legal Abuse Syndrome

off and get the unlawful actions of the local bank out of his life. The suites became ready for tenants.

5. The local bank refused to approve a tenant, a medically oriented health spa. Interest was ticking at $17,000 per month, causing James financial hardship.

6. James retained an attorney who specialized in construction problems. The attorney advised James to file for Chapter 11 reorganization to prevent the bank from foreclosing, as $17,000 per month payments could not continue to be made without the spa tenant's lease payment of $11,000. This would demonstrate to the judge that with the spa tenant in place, the permanent lender could pay off the local lender the full amount of the loan, $1,450,000. Also, this would expose the unreasonableness of the bank refusing to approve the tenant, and the judge would force the bank to treat the estate fairly.

7. James filed with a plan to sell one property to finance the reorganization of his estate.

8. Once in Chapter 11, James was given no opportunity to reorganize. The bank foreclosed and took the building. The building and James' sports bar were given to the contractor for half of the loan amount. All of his other assets were divided between the contractor and the banker.

Legal Abuse Syndrome

9. James sued the bank and the contractor.

10. James' star witness was murdered. This witness had heard the contractor and the banker conspire and was due to testify.

11. A jury trial against the contractor was held like a criminal defense. The attorneys behaved as if their client was guilty. They relied on legal chicanery to defend him. All pertinent evidence was held out by the judge, who cooperated with their outrageous motions. The jury could not be told that the contractor now owned the building and the sports bar. They retired believing that James still owned both. James was slandered, abused, criticized, and harassed by the defense attorneys. Everyone James knew was deposed, even the Methodist minister who had performed his marriage. The jury could not be told the contractor had had his license revoked because he built an unsafe structure without proper permits or inspections. The jury exonerated the guilty criminal out of ignorance.

12. James' hair turned from dark brown to completely gray in 60 days. James' blood pressure was so elevated it required medication, and still does.

It was at this point, seven years after the problem began with the contractor, that James suffered symptoms of Legal Abuse Syndrome.

Events 13 through 15 rendered James helpless in the face of threat to his family and terrorism in his life, and most importantly, profoundly violated his trust in a court system that he believed would protect his rights under the law.

13. Subpoenaed records from the bank proved that the bank's intention was to force James out of business. A competitive spa to be built less than 1000 feet away from James' project was owned by corporate officers of the same bank. James provided evidence to the judge of bank fraud, federal fraud, forgery, perjury, and theft. The crime clearly had been motivated by the need to eliminate James as a competitor. The judge refused to render a decision in the case. Therefore, James' right to appeal was taken from him.

14. The bank maliciously destroyed James' sterling credit standing, and seven attorneys, retained by James in nine years, either cooperated with the bank, or did nothing and drew from the bankruptcy excess funds. When James filed, his worth was $5,000,000 with $2,000,000 in debts, yet he was forced through liquidation. All of James' properties were sold at bargain prices to the contractor and to "friends" of the bank.

15. Fifty-eight efforts have been made to report the crimes to law enforcement agencies, regulators, and those in power. ==No effective response has been elicited==.

All of the above was carefully muddled in mounds of paperwork. Lies, laws, and lawyers wasted a decade of James' life. He moved from hope and confidence to anger, rage, outrage, and determination, until finally James was driven beyond rage, when the judge refused to adjudicate after holding James in painful limbo for three years. The judge responded, "I have problems with that judgment." The lost decade in court is added to the twenty years that it took James to build his estate. James began to sleep with the T.V. on all night. His fine sense of humor was stilled. Alcohol and the couch were his evening companions. He was defensive and not nice. He blamed himself. His view of life became cynical. James' wife describes him as seeming like he'd been struck in the head by a wrecking ball. This was the point of implosion.

Chapter 2

The Epidemic

Legal Abuse Syndrome
A Post Traumatic Stress Disorder

"Injustice anywhere is a threat to justice everywhere."
Dr. Martin Luther King, Jr.

It Doesn't Matter

It doesn't matter that I'm a taxpayer.

It doesn't matter that I'm an American citizen.

It doesn't matter that I'm a law abiding person.

It doesn't matter that I was ripped-off, violated, and betrayed.

It doesn't matter that I was right.

It doesn't matter that I don't hurt other people.

It doesn't matter that I have the evidence.

It doesn't matter that the other person broke the law.

It doesn't matter that he or she is clearly guilty.

It doesn't matter that he or she is clearly wrong by all moral standards.

It doesn't matter that my life is ruined.

It doesn't matter that a Constitution exists.

It doesn't matter that I'm living like a fugitive in my own country.

It doesn't matter that I'm a loyal employee.

It doesn't matter that I gave my life to the company.

It doesn't matter that I'm a veteran who offered his life for his country.

It doesn't matter that I paid more in attorney and legal fees than I earned this year.

It doesn't matter that I told the truth.

LAS victims, bound in cellophane, speak from a fractured consciousness. Helplessness and hopelessness replace outrage driven to the extreme. The majority of people, who contribute to their communities and abide by the law, assume that decent behavior buys them a certain credibility as a good citizen. James found himself slandered and portrayed as a bum and a thief. The shattering of these beliefs sends victims emotionally reeling. These are the macroscopic germs of a national mental health epidemic. Dennis Charny at Yale University reports that uncontrollable stress causes post traumatic stress disorder (PTSD), and the more intense and longer stress lasts, the more likely it is to develop. We know that PTSD doesn't occur in all victims and is more likely to occur if the victim hasn't had the opportunity to work through the crisis (Goleman).

However, the very nature of litigation in today's system requires years of a victim's lifetime. Trauma is reintroduced and remains alive, at least in memory, during the entire court process. At this point the psycholegal aspect enters the clinical picture. How do we know that we really have post traumatic stress disorder versus just feeling bad? Physical changes take place in the brain.

Catastrophic stress alters three key brain circuits (Goleman). The locus ceruleus (see figure 3) regulates brain hormones called catecholamines that help us prepare for emergencies. When the locus ceruleus becomes hyperreactive, it secretes too much brain chemical, and over reacts to small stimuli, which in reality is nonthreatening. Victims startle when they encounter such things as a:

- doorbell ringing
- phone ringing
- sudden noise or movement coming into their awareness

The hypothalamus and pituitary gland regulate stress-response hormones. Activation causes an increase in corticotropin-releasing-factor (CRF). When CRF is released, it mobilizes the body to meet emergencies. The victim's body stays on alert.

- The victim trusts nothing or no one.
- There may be sleep disturbances or changes in sleep posture.
- Obsessions about security, money, privacy, and contracts are common.

The opioid system blunts pain when it registers strong emotion. This system includes the hypothalamus, locus ceruleus, and amygdala.

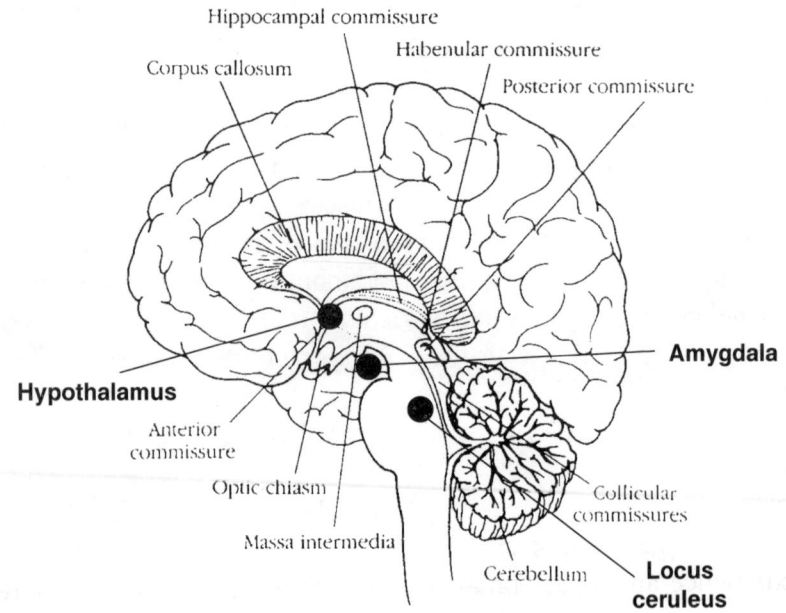

Figure 3 - The Human Brain

- The victim no longer feels passion.
- There are often disorders of sex life.
- Intimate relationships are affected and can complicate family support when it is needed most.
- The victim may be unable to cry or laugh.

PTSD is proving to be pervasive. The American Psychiatric Association reports that one in ten Americans have suffered PTSD, mostly from violent assault (Goleman). When invisible assaults are added, the statistics become mind-boggling. It can masque as voter apathy. It causes us to appear to be a violent nation without tolerance and without forgiveness. The roots of this invisible epidemic are found in the "it doesn't matter's."

The Etiology of Legal Abuse Syndrome

PTSD has existed, unrecognized in victims, for years. Except for PTSD victims from war experience, it was not commonly diagnosed. The psycholegal dimension added to PTSD, creating Psycholegal PTSD or what I have termed LAS, presents a complex clinical picture. Counselors may not recognize the ongoing source(s) of trauma. After the initial assault, psycholegal factors compile to a point of psychobiological change. Further complicating the condition, victims do not always experience every post trauma phase. Some victims experience shock and some do not. All victims experience an impact phase wherein anger and anxiety express themselves in some form. Recoil is followed by post trauma stress symptoms interfacing with post crime activities. Months after the incident, counselors and victims will feel foiled in their attempts to attain symptom-free status when wrestling with psycholegal PTSD.

A mythical "real man" will see the condition more as a matter of character than a mental health issue and, subsequently, try to hide his vulnerability. This is especially true when an influential businessman, who has wielded clout in the community for years, finds himself victimized. He will take the "leave me alone, there's nothing wrong with me" attitude. This is self-doubt and depression speaking.

Bashing from business assaults is given wide berth among business people. Keen, *Fire in the Belly*, writes that "when we live within the horizons of the economic myth, we begin to consider it honorable for a man to do whatever he must to make a living...we tailor our personality to what the market requires." Men will say that injustice is "simply how the system works" and will be led to believe that enduring court madness is just part of today's business. When these men finally sit in therapy, they cry out for the moral code that has been violated.

Victims find that outrage is common. Anger, whether displaced or appropriately focused, finds little therapeutic direction. Self-blame and self-doubt are also common. Depression from helplessness and isolation follows. Further untreated, psycholegal PTSD becomes chronic.

Guilt is part of the comforting process and victims will cling to it. That is why therapists and friends are advised to refrain from saying, "You have nothing to feel guilty about." Victims of deceptive assaults, followed by legal injustice, are candidates for raw, throbbing, inflamed, existential guilt. That means they are, by their very existence, guilty and shamed. When a child turns to his or her parent for validation of good behavior, he expects protection against bullies and violators.

Children depend, at a basic ego level, on the parent's support and sanction of good versus evil along with protection. If the parent turns his back on the child and joins with the abuser, it invalidates the child's sense of rightness and wrongness. Such an episode creates a mental health crisis in that child. Existential shame and guilt is forever etched on that human being's ego. Those who suffer such shame don't just make errors; they *are the error*.

Adults are vulnerable to existential shame as well. The entire legalized interpretation of right and wrong leaves goodness not sanctioned by society in any meaningful way. The business bullies, who hire teams of attorneys that function more like legal street gangs, use the law to merely take and run, regardless of precedent. When pinstripe becomes a gang color, the laws get turned inside out against the very population they are instituted to protect. They assault by verbal abuse and paper takings instead of drive-by shootings, but are no less gangsters than the bullies in street gangs. Judges who cooperate with the "unactionable" abuses turn their backs instead of responding to their sworn trust, which is to represent society in the battle of goodness vs. badness. Adult shaming is the result. Existential guilt is a factor to be dealt with in every phase of recovery from deceptive assault (Tucker, Bard).

Those who are around the victim are profoundly affected. Children of victims become cynical about their lives. Mates absorb the defensiveness and are also victimized. Helpers can only walk through post crime trauma as a supportive, directive force. If the victim faces litigation, he or she must be prepared for years of front-line battle.

> James spent $140,000 on legal fees and costs. (All were new moneys he'd earned after everything was taken.) He received nothing in return. Additionally, he spent seven years painfully reliving traumatic memories while gathering evidence and preparing his case.

The victim can minimize the chances of LAS by preparing for and processing each assault as it is delivered. Sequelae are varied in each victim's case, but the eight steps, outlined in the following chapters, have proven to be helpful tools for managing and recovering from the wide range of trauma that he will face. The best way to avoid LAS is to ensure justice. Victims need to influence the injurers in order to reaffirm the moral law. Any experiences that support this endeavor, such as a fair trial and appropriate punishment, based on the victim's testimony, can resolve the matter and prevent LAS. It is impossible to divorce the moral and psychological issues from the legal activities if the victim is to emerge with satisfying closure.

By continually denying justice, LAS will become contagious. All of society's ills are impacted by injustices without proper societal correction. Homelessness (James and his family were homeless for a time), addictions, and "holics" to various substances are typical occurrences. Self-medication is common when emotional pain is suffered in isolation. Divorce and break-up of families are caused by LAS. The family may survive the first assault from the crime, but years of litigation tests the strongest of relationships. Unfocused hatred may render silent bitterness in a victim for a lifetime. Ultimately, for some, suicide is a chosen option because suicide is the ultimate control in a life that is out of control.

Eight Steps to Recovery:

Debriefing
Grieving
Obsession
Blaming
Deshaming
Reframing
Empowerment
Recovery

The Epidemic

Chapter 3

Debriefing

Opening the Can of Worms— A first Step on a Journey

"A friend is one before whom I may think aloud."
R. Waldo Emerson

Debriefing is one of the most simple, inexpensive, and effective techniques that can be applied when stressful events occur. The psychological, physical, spiritual, and societal damage that follows stressful events is cumulative in nature and may take years to manifest in clear symptomatology. Anyone who cares about the victim can do debriefing. It all starts with quality listening.

Hans Selye pioneered the work of psychological stress and its effects on human functioning. Emotional disorders, medical syndromes, diminished work performance, and strained family relationships, are recognized areas of concern for those who have jobs with high profile for critical incidence. It has been easy to see potential for trauma in law enforcement staff, crisis team workers, fire fighters, crash crews, and social service personnel. However, all professionals who provide services to the population at large watch the same devastating syndromes in those who have been victimized by crime, who have been part of litigation, or who have been deceptively assaulted. The fact is that whenever events are so profoundly dramatic, shocking, disturbing or long lasting, they exponentially jeopardize one's ability to function effectively.

There seems to be broad agreement that the first step to recovery for post trauma victims requires a complete debriefing from the start, the impact phase of the experience. Direct therapeutic exposure to the traumatic event has been identified as the single most important treatment factor in PTSD (Keane, Reese). How does debriefing help? Therapeutic characteristics of the debriefing experience are modified from Zegan:

1. Debriefing provides a "revisiting" of the experience in a milieu of physical and psychological "safety."

2. It provides an attachment to others who are perceived to be concerned with the individual's survival and recovery.

3. It affiliates the disorganized victim with a clear path of rules, reinforcements, and appropriate intimacy with others.

4. It offers an environment of support and acceptance at a time of pain, shame, and self-blame.

5. It provides coherency with an individual or support group in the midst of a disaster.

Legal Abuse Syndrome

The walking wounded have sustained multiple assaults. Participants do not need to isolate one assault as *the* traumatic injury. Rather than a "bottom line" approach, debriefing allows the accumulation of pain to be brought forth. Bard and Sangrey refer to the three stages of crisis: impact, recoil and reorganization. The walking wounded are stuck in a cycle of the impact/recoil phases while they absorb assaults from the system. As long as they cycle through impact/recoil, reorganization is impossible. Victims state the issues surrounding their distress:

1. Powerlessness - I'm vulnerable.
2. Isolation - I've lost control.
3. Guilt - I have frustrated feelings of responsibility.
4. Hypervigilance - What if it happens again?
5. Numbness - How did this happen to me?
6. Anxiety - I experience aggressive impulses.
7. Startle responses - I suffer emotional lability.
8. Rage - toward respondents, bureaucracies, and courts. I'm suffering from cumulative assaults.
9. Confusion and shame - I question my decisions.
10. Disorientation - My life-style and belief system are in shambles.

Debriefing is Complicated by Common Distortions of Communication (What Helpers Need to Know)

Why is it usually not helpful to share your devastation with your best friends and family? Even though it is so desperately needed in order to begin healing, a strange thing happens when you begin to detail the experience. Helpers' eyes glaze over, cliches roll off the tongues of even the most sensitive, and there is that compulsion in listeners to keep disasters on a positive note. Let's look at two dynamics at work:

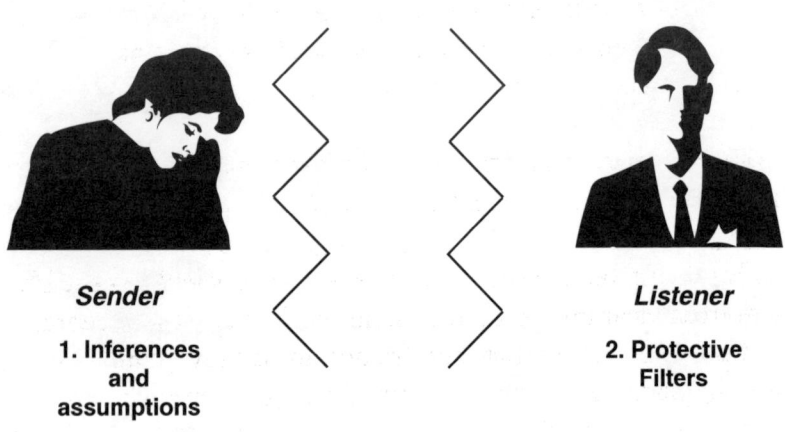

Barriers to Communication

Sender

1. Inferences and assumptions

Listener

2. Protective Filters

1. *Inferences and assumptions* come from each individual's past experiences. The sum total of these create an orientation toward life that will be projected onto others. Very often, the victim has misperceived the perpetrator's intentions and

agenda. If the victim is a trustworthy person, it is natural that he or she will assume trustworthiness in the perpetrator.

2. *Protective filters* are always at work. If an individual begins to share with another and the data threatens the listener's feelings of safety, they may try to divert the data or simply not hear it at all. Denial is found in all of us. Painful data is always tempting to deny. These can turn into outrageous situations, however. The sender may break the message down to kindergarten level and deliver it in his or her clearest and loudest voice only to find that the receiver is momentarily deaf.

The function of this protective filter is to maintain the equilibrium of the listener. Victims' stories shake the foundations that we lean upon in order to feel safe. When it is impossible for friends or family to hear, due to their protective psychological filters shielding them from vicarious pain, the victim feels rejected and alone.

Also, victims find that their friends and family members rarely have the patience or skills to listen thoroughly enough to allow a truly effective debriefing experience. The more nebulous and complicated the crime and its aftermath, the more the listener's eyes will glaze over as the victim shares. Uncomfortable listeners will also pitch in and try to solve the problem. They will actively help the victim to "find a solution" or change the way he or she feels. Such self serving efforts are not helpful and even add to the victim's frustration.

Then there will be the victim-blamers. It has been the style to blame the victim for centuries. Victims are distasteful in their losing posture and frightening to face. How does this "blame the victim" myth perpetuate? Victim-blamers find an easy explanation of the crimes, causing themselves to feel safer. If it is the victim's fault, then the rest of us are not at risk. Too bad that such explanations are mythical and often a delusional and self-deceptive way of coping with discomfort.

The stylish "unconscious-motivation" concept stemmed from the psychoanalytic theory in which masochism, in close relationships, caused one party to set himself up for suffering. The theory is that "love hurts." Later, the victim role was portrayed as a manipulative game that some people would play in their personal interactions (Bern). None of these theories can be born out in personal-crime victim circumstances. Most importantly, crime victims must not be treated as though they are "guilty until proven innocent." A debriefing process is offered to ensure a constructive, helpful response to LAS victims.

The Debriefing Process
The Center Circle

If debriefing is done in a group, each participant should have several Debriefing Worksheets. Divide the group into dyads or pairs. One member of the dyad is a listener and one shares his story. Then, when finished, the roles are reversed.

On the worksheet, you will see a center circle surrounded by bigger circles divided into sections. The major, initial impact experience is written in the center circle. Then the significant resulting cumulative assaults or "ripple effects" are written in adjacent sections. All players are listed and named and the events are portrayed as if a picture was being painted in words.

Two people can effectively handle the debriefing experience by each taking turns being the sender and the listener. Debriefing is best done with a counselor or support group since breakthroughs in denial are common during this experience. Either the victim or listener might break through denial at any time. It is helpful to have a supportive person or group at that time.

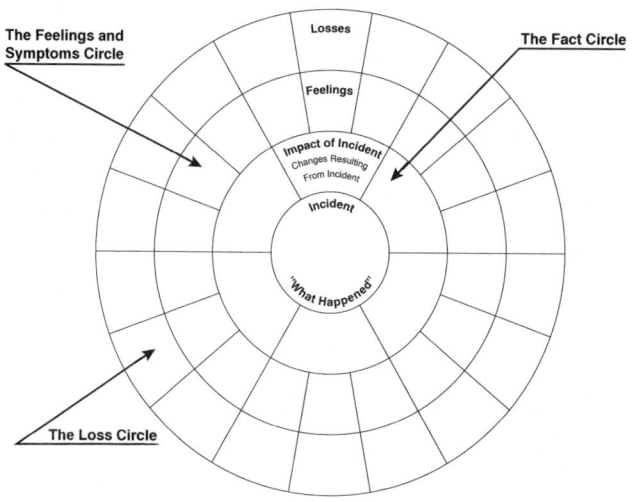

Figure 4 - The Debriefing Worksheet *

If the victim feels uncomfortable with another person and cannot be in a supportive experience, some degree of debriefing can be done alone. Take each step slowly and be prepared to respond to each of the lead-ins below. Don't "white knuckle" it. Don't force yourself to endure brutal pain without a break. Be supportive and

---

* See appendix D for worksheets.

caring with yourself as you would be with another person. If you need to cry, it might be good to be with someone who will hug you and care, even if you choose not to share the specific data.

Look again at the debriefing sheets. The initial event is now written in the center. After the initial impact, begin the fact circle.

The Fact Circle

After the initial impact event has been written in the center of the <u>debriefing sheet</u>, you begin a cognitive process. Answer the following in the fact circle:

> What happened?
>
> Who did it?
>
> Where was each person in each event?
>
> What was said, as close to quotes as possible?
>
> When did each event take place?
>
> Who were co-victims, family members, business associates or others whose lives were dramatically effected by the assault?

Mark the events that still feel the most outrageous with some symbol and key it at the bottom of the page. If misinformation was introduced, underscore it.

The Feeling and Symptoms Circle

Next, as the sender, add feelings and emotional experiences in the designated circle. Include all physical, mental, and emotional symptoms. You are not expected to clinically diagnose PTSD or LAS. The cognitive and emotional aspects of debriefing are not designed to ascertain or rule out a clinical diagnosis of post trauma stress. Variables abound in such an endeavor and it is assumed that all traumatic events will yield a measure of post traumatic stress. Whether an event is merely unsettling, but tolerable, or, at the other end of the continuum, has disrupted his life and left the victim devastated, we will all benefit more if we err on the side of establishing healing processes for minor pain than if we do "too little too late."

A thesis of this book is that we, as a society, compound trauma and offer little in the way of comfort or efficient response to victims of deceptive assault and post litigation or post crime trauma. Another function of this book is to take the reader through steps to recovery that can be ventured alone or in a group. Whether alone or supported by others, the following lead-ins will help to develop the emotional/symptom part of the debriefing sheet, the first major step in the ritual to recovery.

Answer again and again in terms of emotional reactions:

"And then what..?"

"And then how were you feeling?"

The listener helps to expand on the feelings by reflecting:

"Sounds like..."

"You felt as if...."

"From your point of view or perception..."

"It felt as if..."

"It seemed as if life..."

You can ask yourself...

"At that point I just felt like..."

"The whole world seemed..."

"I felt like I needed..."

"In my deepest heart I felt..."

"My sleep became..."

The Loss Circle (material and non-material)

The next step is to identify losses in detail - material and nonmaterial - including losses to society as a whole. Victims are very sensitive about the expansive nature of their experiences. Society's losses are sorely felt by responsible victims. Write your losses in the circle.

1. First fill the circle with material losses: property, money, and treasures; then, move on to nonmaterial losses.

2. List at least 3 beliefs, and more if you can, that represent losses of your belief system. These key into trust issues.

   "What did I believe before the event(s)?"

   "What do I believe now?"

   "What is happening as a result of the experience?"

   "What should be happening?"

3. Next comes the philosophical and spiritual side of the losses:

   "Why me?"

   Who has been affected?

   How do you explain the crime or assault, if you can?

   Do you relate it to past "bad" behavior?

   Do you blame yourself?

   How deep does the damage go?

   "To what am I vulnerable?"

   "What can I not control?" (List on back of Worksheet)*

   "What can I control?" (List on back of Worksheet)*

   What feelings have changed?

---

* Refer to *appendix D* for worksheets.

Talk about the moral law that was violated.

Do you feel abandoned by God?

What losses to society as a whole exist from this experience?

Perspective for Helpers

Being helpful to a victim is not an easy task whether you're a professional in the helping services or not. We must be willing to accept anything the offended relates. Acceptance doesn't mean that we approve, only accept. Listening and caring provides a moment of clarification and expression for the victim. The offended needs his or her full range of traumatic experience to be heard in an accepting environment. Refusal, by the listener, to believe the worst of what he hears, is the work of the perceptual filter. That filtering function, which lends comfortable closure to traumatic data for the listener, devastates the sender.

Glazed eyes and inability to grasp profound injustices not only reject the victim's experience, but such denial can have grave societal impact. We don't report, testify, face, and effectively deal with what we refuse to acknowledge. Certainly, the ability to prevent victimization is effected by first confronting its existence.

The listener should expect to become uncomfortable. Criminal or deceptive behavior creates distrust in everyone. A single crime will birth more than one victim. Everyone who must face the story will be emotionally and economically affected as part of society. It is said that every crime has two victims, the offended party and society as a whole. Seminar participants share that even vicarious crimes on the nightly news cause distress.

Debriefing is a forum where the victim is free from suspicion, slander, doubt, and the self-protecting perceptive filter of most listeners. During debriefing, there is no evaluation or critical response. Every statement is accepted and reflected in such a way that it finds its place on debriefing sheets, causing the victim to feel heard and validated. It is irrelevant whether or not we believe the victim. It is most relevant that we believe in the victim and his perceptions of the events. As well, the process assures the victim that recovery is possible.

Listeners need to refrain from fixing, suggesting, or trying to solve at this stage. The listeners must be willing to validate the injured person's experience of injury, allow compassionate and caring responses, and help the injured put the events in order. Remind yourself that the victim owns the problem. We are there for them and with them, that's all. There is no question that brutal honesty with one's own vulnerability is difficult to face, but once accomplished, it becomes an investment in empowerment.

It was only after a $140,000 expenditure on legal fees and devastation at the hands of attorneys that James saw, through dashed dreams, that his cherished vision of justice through the courts was a myth. Not only did it ruin his enjoyment of *Perry Mason* and *L.A. Law*, he had to face that such delusional beliefs had destroyed his life-style. Even more importantly, he concluded that mythical beliefs regarding justice, held by much of the population, left his country at risk. He decided that if he did not take the reins and attempt to force his court system to work, as the law provides, that the country he valued leaving to his children would not exist. Unfortunately, the reality of the system came after attorney and court abuses had taken such a large toll in money and time that his rights as a citizen can never be fully realized. Nevertheless, pro se, James is continuing his fight out of principle and sheer determination. This will be shared in more detail in later chapters.

More Hints for Helpers:

- Do not mirror.
- Don't be objective.
- Don't play devil's advocate.
- Don't teach.
- Don't analyze.

As the victim admits, explores, and talks, the job is to find out what happened and to whom he or she is hostage. The debriefing sheet helps to pinpoint the injuries and the injurers. Until he claims the injury and therapeutically blames the injurer, he cannot balance the scales and let go. Real offenders will emerge as the processing occurs. Sometimes this will have an element of surprise. A sense of control begins to return when we know the "who and what."

Absolutely What Not to Say to A Victim

1. "You must forgive and forget."
   Maybe he will forgive in his time; he will never forget.

2. "It's only money."
   Money reflects the victim's status, feelings of worth, security, earned life-style and taste. Every item is a part of the inner person.

3. "There are two sides to every story."
   When a crime is committed, there may be two sides, but one side can be dead wrong. The victim is not responsible for both sides, only a healthy resolution of his side.

4. "I know just how you feel." "I <u>care</u> how you feel," *is better.*

5. "I believe you." "I believe <u>in</u> you," *is better.*

6. "You still have your health/ kids/ family."
   Kids, family and health opposed to material goods are apples and oranges. One does not solve the other. The mourner does not have to bargain. "Take my money, just don't let my kids get sick or die." The victim does not need to subordinate loss of property in his emotional experience. He is entitled to all of it.

7. "You're young, you can start over."
   His youth did not belong to a criminal.

8. "It's not as bad as it seems."
   Imagine how lonely a victim feels to know how bad it is and to have the other unwilling to see it. It may be every bit as bad as it seems and it might get worse from there. <u>Who</u> can't bear to believe it is this bad? The listener is self-serving here. This statement rejects the victim's experience.

9. "Crying isn't going to help anything."
   We don't cry to help things. We cry because nothing helps. It is the natural response. If the victim doesn't cry and grieve, he will become depressed. Depression lasts longer than mourning.

10. "You're not alone."
    We are all in this alone. Better is "I'm beside you." The experience is the victim's alone.

11. Regarding crimes of the heart, "I know he/she really loves you."
    Love is not a reliable indicator of healthy relationships. Let's settle for being treated well and not being deceived.

12. "You should have..."
    These are efforts for the listener to feel better by finding what the victim did wrong. These responses cause further guilt in the victim. The victim did not cause the crime.

13. "Why didn't you...?"
    No one needs any criticism, ever. The victim has endlessly replayed the incident and knows every option he or she "should" have taken.

14. "There are starving people..." "It could have been worse."
    The better anything gets, the more one misses it when it's gone. Others' misfortunes are not comforting, only more distressing.

15. "You can't let yourself be obsessed by this...it's all you think about."
    You cannot not be obsessed. Obsession is a healthy reaction to trying to get one's life back in control. Society has been helped by the obsessions of offended people. Look at what MADD (Mothers Against Drunk Driving) has done for highway safety.

16. "He'll get his someday." "What goes around comes around."
    Maybe so, but it never comes around fast enough. Some spiritual and religious beliefs can be comforting if the victim truly believes. When trust has been shattered, it is as hard to trust God as it is life.

17. "That's just how the system works." "It's the best system in the world."
    This condones outrage and ridiculousness. We're not comparing lousy systems. This one happens to owe us as taxpayers an honest response to crime that punishes wrong and rewards right.

18. "It's only business."
    - ✓ *This assumes ethics and morals aren't to be expected in business dealings. Greed and power are accepted as revered ruling forces. Cissela Bok in her book on lying quotes, "Even the devils themselves do not lie to one another, since the society of Hell could not subsist without truth any more than others." Samuel Johnson (BOK)*

19. "Don't cry over spilled milk."
    "Spilled milk" is a loss. There is no more appropriate time to cry than when one has experienced a loss.

The cases of James and others will be revisited as the rigors of each step to recovery are shared by these courageous victims.

The Case Study of P.J.

P.J. is a psychologist. She is educated, bright, mature and widely experienced as a salesperson and former teacher. P.J. attended one of my seminars and, during the description of the debriefing process, she began to sob. The breakthrough in denial occurred as the presentation developed. For more than a decade, she had suppressed feelings and absorbed cumulative assaults from a criminal relative and the system.

The relative had borrowed $5,000 from her. When the loan was due, he paid her in stock that he represented was worth $8,000. He wrote a personal guarantee that he would pay her $12,000 if the stock had not reached the promised amount in a given number of years. She was convinced. She also believed in the company the stock represented. The purpose of the company was to produce a versatile, high-efficiency, low pollution fuel. A few years later, there was a merger with another company. P.J. never received her new stock certificates, only promises, stalls, and lies from the relative.

P.J. began contacting governmental agencies. The securities commissions of Nevada, Arizona, and California all claimed the other had jurisdiction. P.J. lived in Nevada, the first company was in Arizona and the new company was in California. The securities commissions all advised her to get an attorney. She was unable to meet the financial demands of the attorneys that she consulted. She then tried to locate other victims of the same scam in hopes they could share fees. That was to no avail. The state attorney general told her to contact consumer affairs. Consumer Affairs told her to contact the FBI. The FBI did nothing. P.J. wrote to her Congressmen and they wrote back token responses ending with, "If there is anything we can do, let us know." She found herself being recycled through agencies only to have them refer her to other agencies.

All along, she tried to confront the relative. He rationalized every time. She could not get a straight answer, and to make it worse, her mother died. Somehow, the same relative arrived on the scene with

> paperwork that allowed him to inherit all that was left of her parents' estate.
>
> She became ill and was diagnosed with cancer. P.J. remains bright, alive and aware, but she is now disabled. She states, "I have time on my hands to churn over this outrage. I fear that I will die an angry soul."

P.J.'s story reflects the pain fermenting over years with no place to turn. The "rip-off" relative conned the rest of the family, so P.J. had no family with whom to share her anger or who cared to hear her. Twelve years of denying her anger and shutting down to accommodate a family who would not listen to her speak badly about a relative caused P.J. to suffer alone and stifle her feelings.

A simple description of the condition and the debriefing process stimulated her into a breakthrough in her denial and validated her sense of outrage. It was the first step toward pardoning her life sentence as "an angry soul." She had been made to feel ashamed for her wrath and forced to pretend she was not enraged when attending family functions. P.J. was in a lose-lose trap. On the one hand, she would lose her family if she was honest with herself and them; on the other, P.J. would lose herself in terms of her integrity if she was not honest about her victimization. She remained in a lose-lose limbo for twelve years. An unspectacular crime and an invisible victim are so easy to deny and to bury in a day's activities. The rage within then eats away at the victim's total existence.

What To Do With the Worms After the Can is Open

Fear of opening up the whole traumatic issue of victimization prevents us from being comfortable with debriefing experiences as well. Those around the victim become frustrated by the burden of negative information and the fact that there is often little we can do to solve the problem itself. Friends and family are fearful that they may lack the skills to deal with psychological issues, if they emerge. Certainly, some participants will require professional mental health services. But instead of fearing the debriefing process, we need to realize that it is the facilitator of a transition to greater mental health.

First, however, the victim needs to be guided toward a well defined process. The steps to recovery, as outlined in the following chapters, provide the follow-up to debriefing. We fear the worms that might crawl out of the can. We are shocked by their vileness in the can and we are nonplused as to what to do with the creatures. The eight steps prepare us to greet emotions and behaviors that come forth. Instead of worms that seek blindly to be fulfilled, victims are gently guided toward actions. They grasp realities and skills propelling them from the hostage relationship into which they've been cast. Listening, caring, and being there as this journey begins become a privilege, a challenge and a pleasure.

Chapter 4

Grieving
A Life Skill that Insures Longevity

> *"Unlike life, death cannot be taken away from man,
> and therefore we may consider it is the gift of God."*
> Seneca (Letting Go With Love)

One's own death is thought to be the greatest loss that a person can sustain. Death of a loved one is thought to be in second place (O'Connor). Poets and philosophers ponder death in view of the fact that each person relates to death through unique spiritual beliefs. One thing we know for sure is that death is imminent. It is equal opportunity and it is random. Death might render our final reward for good deeds, it may be a total nothingness or mete out eternal suffering in Hell. It is the finality of a life; it is a time when one is remembered and eulogized in the funeral, one of life's ceremonies of passage.

No such romantic pondering is done about loss resulting from criminal betrayal. No spiritual belief supports it, nor is philosophical print likely to intrigue a person into feeling it might be a wonderful surprise after all. It seems to me that as painful as it may be, death is not the most devastating loss a person can sustain. Rather, the most profound loss is loss of trust, especially loss of trust in those who are the guardians of our protection, our vital rights and our privileges. Loss of a mate due to betrayal of a trust or loss of trust in a parent looms larger in terms of anguish than their deaths. Likewise, for Americans, loss of trust in the government as a protective system of checks and balances cannot be buried and mourned, leaving behind good and nostalgic memories. The victim is in prolonged grief without transcendence.

The Story of Judy

There sat an intense, slight blond woman in her thirties. The tone of her voice combined hysteria and disbelief. She had been a single mother with two children for several years. She had met and fallen in love with a bright and ambitious financial consultant. Judy related how her heart had gone out to him when he told of the deaths of his mother and father in a boating accident in the East. Judy married him. She designed their home to comfort this orphaned survivor.

The children called him "daddy" and, for the first time in years, she described her life as "happy." The relationship felt stable and they celebrated their second anniversary. Judy remembers the brisk morning in September when she drove the children to school in her new Lincoln. She had helped her husband get credit since he was new to town.

She arrived back at home, making a mental shopping list as she got out of the car. Three cars with four men in each pulled up in front of her house. Curious, thinking they were Realtors on a tour, she greeted them and was handed a search warrant. The 12 FBI agents combed her house and informed her that the man she married didn't exist. He had assumed 3 identities in his life of white-collar crime. Judy was in shock. She didn't easily lose trust in people.

From jail, her husband told her he'd been a government witness and there must have been a mistake. They put up $50,000 and he was let out of jail pending trial. She vowed to stand by him if he was truthful. They pledged their finances to his defense.

It was early morning when Judy came to the kitchen. She knew her husband was up, and came to talk if he needed. A letter was on the kitchen table telling her good-by and that the car was on the 3rd level of the airport parking structure. All of their money was gone too.

Numbness, confusion, disbelief, protest and denial rule the victim's life. There is a betrayal. It is thrust on the offended who then feels raw and severed from the familiar. Profound sadness gushes up through the body spontaneously. Life is changed.

The reality of her grief presented a tragic picture for Judy. Her love was real and her commitment sound. If her husband had died, friends would have surrounded her with food, flowers and phone calls, and a funeral would have been the focus; a tremendous loss for sure but a loss with a therapeutic ritual and fond memories that keep love alive.

Instead of a comforting ritual, a passage that leaves one rich from experience, Judy was in a lose-lose "no man's land." She bore the loss with varying responses from friends and family. Some were suspicious of her. Law enforcement officials and friends implicated her in the crimes. Some couldn't resist the "I told you so" or "I knew there was... something about him."

> The FBI continued to question Judy and it became obvious that she was in jeopardy of being legally accused as a co-conspirator. Her "husband's" business partners began to harass Judy because they too had been "ripped off." One sued to get her house. Her credit was in jeopardy. And, of course, last on the scene was the IRS. They audited her records and informed her that she would have to pay the non-person's taxes.
>
> Judy stayed in an impact/loss/recoil cycle for nearly two years. She sold personal items, her jewelry and furniture, and tried to work. Judy wanted an annulment since her marriage had been fraudulent. She retained an attorney. It was her belief that the retainer was the fee to get an annulment. When she went before the judge, he informed her that she could get a divorce but there was not adequate case law presented to allow her an annulment. Her attorney called her outside the courtroom and told her that for another $1450 he could get the annulment. She took the divorce.

Judy was still terrorized that she might be indicted for the crimes of her "non-husband" when an interesting twist to the tale arose. FBI agents questioned her repeatedly throughout the weeks after the disappearance. One agent became so detailed that he asked about her eating and drinking habits. He learned that she ate a blue cheese dip every evening while watching TV. Laboratory analysis turned up traces of phenobarbital in the dip. While she slept, soundly drugged, her husband had made small holes in the wall where the products of his clandestine activities were stored.

Grieving feels like a waste of time and energy to invisible victims. Their survival is on the line and they usually think that they don't have time for crying or feeling sad. They treat themselves with impatience. At this point, victims will castigate themselves for crying, feeling sad, or not maintaining a productive life as though they were not in grief. They will say during their counseling sessions, "I'm sorry (for crying)," "I thought I was doing okay," "I'm not doing well," or "Why can't I get over this?" In fact they are doing well. They are crying normally and reacting as they honestly feel, in grief. It is important to look back at the debriefing sheet and identify the losses in the loss circle. When we do this, it is no wonder that the victim is crying. It helps to look at the loss circle and identify specific losses which hurt the most at the time of tears. Grieving is serious business and must be seen as such by the victim, therapists, friends and family, and the courts.

Health & Behavior Hazards to the LAS Victim in Grief

Facts show that victims in grief are at risk. They are more accident prone and more vulnerable to illnesses. Grief softens the immune system. Stress related illness, even cancer, is more likely during grief. It was after the loss of family relationships, belief in any of the established systems, and material goods that P.J. succumbed to bone cancer. For the first time in his life as he sank into the feelings of helplessness in his efforts to find justice, James' hair turned gray and he developed hypertension that required medication. Judy couldn't swallow. She lost nineteen pounds in three weeks. Her legs shook and she had muscle spasms. Her face broke out in more than blemishes; they were open sores. She had a profound sense that she was dying. Hives came and went. It also seems that right at the time reports need to be filed and information related to law enforcement, attorneys, or others, the victim may have memory lapses. This protective function of denial now becomes a complication in the attempt to attain justice. Defense attorneys and law enforcement officers attack any mental confusion. Attorneys' adversarial manner and impatience to get at facts over feelings perpetuates the victim's deterioration. Invalidation of the victim's stories adds to the victim's feelings of shame and guilt. Suicide is often fantasized.

If evil intent is behind the deceptive actions, the trauma is manyfold as great as if the devastation is random. One loss begets another. In a legal fight, the attack on assets as well as person sets up the strategic abuse of due process. Malice aforethought or the planned and executed devastation of another human being, in order to weaken him in court wars, is standard operating procedure.

Litigants, victims of white-collar crime, and victims of deceptive rip-offs find themselves in a never-ending life style in which they face risk of loss or actual loss of status, property, and community respect at varying magnitudes every day. Full frontal assault, battle conditions, and wild outrage are simply strategy-as-usual for those who buy into today's legal games. When we know courts are involved, there is usually a direct pipeline from assaults to tangible and intangible losses.

Takings - Legalized Robbery

Now we come to "takings." Takings have to do with powerful organizations, governments, agencies, and/or enforcement officials having the power to take private property purportedly for the purpose of enforcing the law, a regulation, or somehow acting in the line of duty. The IRS can effect takings as can the DEA. The bankruptcy court reflects systematized takings (Brooks Hearings, Appendix C). Courts often uphold takings even though the 5th amendment clearly prohibits taking of private property in excess of $20 for the public good without just compensation and never without due process. Takings are methods of stealing that are concealed in procedural confusion. Savings and loans who "went broke" did so because takings occurred at the top. Depositors who couldn't withdraw their life's savings were nonetheless ripped off (Kusic).

Each and every person who is victimized directly or indirectly by a taking will experience deep and immutable grief. Removal of property violates all rights, all decency. Takings impact all dimensions of a victim's life. The assault resounds through relationships, the physical self, spiritual beliefs, and future performance. If malice aforethought is part of the removal of property, we know from Bev Flanigan's book, *Forgiving the Unforgivable*, the victim is taken emotional hostage and the grief is intensified. Yet, victims feel confused about takings because the right and wrong cannot be clearly established.

The Case Study of John

John, a stocky older man, sat in my office sobbing so hard that his shoulders heaved and tears ran off the end of his nose. The half-box of tissue he'd used was partially wadded and dropped and part was still squeezed between his hands and eyes. He was crying over the death of his gerbil. Due to being evicted from his home, the gerbil was overheated in his cage while being transported to his new "home." I had a hunch there was more to the story than the death of a pet. Obviously, John could not have presented this issue outside of the therapist's office. He had to start with what hurt and was the easiest to tell. However, underlying every presenting problem will be other dynamics, and therapy allows us the luxury of opening the doors to those underlying problems.

John has been one of many over the past 20 years who seemingly entered therapy presenting a grief issue that the normal public would have considered an insignificant loss in the overall scheme of things. By the time John's case developed, a familiar theme began to take shape. John shared that he was a veteran. He'd committed his life to

America's freedom during one of the wars and had served his country with honor.

He had come out of the service and begun his own business as a mason. He'd done well over the years and had come to care for a bright young man who had worked for him for ten years. Recession hit and John had some business reversals, but they weren't bad.

His attorney, whom he'd used over many years and whom he trusted, suggested that he place his business in Chapter 11 bankruptcy in order to reorganize his debts to ease his debt burden. John ✓ acted on his attorney's advice. His attorney's actions then placed more burden upon John than the original debt load. Properties were being removed from John's estate and his attorney was cooperating with the destruction of the estate.

A taking is occurring. John is suffering the losses of properties and finally his home, but he has never cried over such things. He's an ex-army man who will come out fighting and has no time for tears. He's been witness to worse destruction, buddie's lives shattered into bits and other battle-born trauma. "This is a business problem not worth crying over." But when the debriefing was completed, John was a victim. His belief system was devastated and further complicated by malice aforethought.

At the battlefront, it is critical to believe that the horror of war is endured for some meaningful reason. America, all that it stands for, freedom and opportunity were at the core of John's persona. He lived the American dream and that idealism shored him up in the face of danger. John was a good, pragmatic businessman and not an idealist to a fault. He thought that when a professional person was hired to do a job within the scope of his profession that some ethical standard was imposed upon the actions of the professional. Therefore, after years of good service from his attorney, reviewing contracts, writing letters, handling a will and trusts, he believed that he had a competent professional to turn to when he was in financial trouble. That assumption precluded knowledge of how the court system in America has evolved. For John, this belief set him up to be victimized by malice aforethought complicated by trust.

Where and How Takings Occur

How do lawyers fit into the grief style of the invisible victim? Lawyers are the gatekeepers of the court system. As author David Marston put it in *Malice Aforethought*, "As you already know if you have ever glanced at your bank loan agreement or apartment lease or any other legalese in your life, definitions do for lawyers what morning coffee does for everyone else; we can't get started without them." Lawyers are in every part of every business telling people about various definitions of laws and rules. While attorneys are also

Legal Abuse Syndrome

guided by ethical rules, a strange evolution has taken place in the legal business. Ethical rules are written to protect lawyers and it seems that lawyers function either to take advantage of this, or at least to turn their heads the other way when ethical rules are violated, says Marston. This leaves lawyers neck-deep in the "taking" business and those lawyers who take no action allow the profession to deteriorate. The many lawyers and judges who are fine professionals find themselves victimized by the abusers as well. Marston's perspective focuses on those who breach their ethics, the worst of the profession. He tells us that, generalized, lawyers who abuse fall into four categories:

1. Lawyers who use their legal training to break the law or commit crimes in the course of their practice.

2. Lawyers who violate any <u>important</u> ethical rule of the legal profession. Not surprisingly, there are big rules and little rules and lots of technicalities, so the focus here will be on <u>significant</u> professional misconduct, not minor infractions.

3. Lawyers who use their legal training to do things they should be ashamed to tell their mothers.

4. Lawyers who cooperate when they know there is a bad lawyer at work. Such lawyers may go through the steps but will not go up against the system on behalf of his client. These, Marston calls "Unindicted co-conspirators."

Our cases portray Marston's brutal assessment of attorneys. Quite apart from the original assaults, their attorneys added outrage to trauma. It can be hard to identify such slick malice aforethought, but it is there, buried in legalese, and the grieving process will be profoundly compounded by it. Professionals are retained for their good service. Trust is on the line. When such trust is betrayed, intense grief with a pipeline to basic beliefs cannot be avoided.

Skilled Grieving

Rarely is quality grieving done in isolation. Without the ability to recognize and communicate the intricacies that make up depth, tone, and totality of the victim's losses, the griever will be left unsupported by misunderstanding. It is critical to study the loss circle on the debriefing sheet. Invisible victims soon learn that losses of possessions are minimized by our society. No ritual exists for processing grief over loss of one's home, properties, businesses and other "things." The victim is treated with impatience if much emotion is displayed while grieving over material goods. So the offended denounces his emotions, not wanting to appear to feel sorry for himself. He subordinates pain to: (1) "luck" that health may be marginally intact, (2) "kids are okay", and (3) the endless "it could have been worse"-isms. People function rather normally around the victims as if zombiehood is an okay state of being. Wrong!

Personal property symbolizes who we are. Possessions are the outward manifestations of our inner identity. We are surrounded by those items which represent an earned life style, a birthright in America, part of our pursuit of happiness, the expression of our-

selves, and that which we shape to pass on to our posterity.
Losses grieved include:

- Property
- Opportunity
- Relationships
- Money
- Material possessions
- Credit
- Social standing
- Pride
- Patriotism
- "American dream"
- Family
- Home
- Pets
- Time
- Friends
- Reputation
- Businesses
- Borrowing power
- Networking power
- Health
- Earned life style
- Trust/faith
- Law suits filed for recovery
- Hope
- Faith in any protective agency
- Faith in public servants
- Faith in professionals
- Life's time, critical time to move ahead or rebuild

The walking wounded, LAS victims, are grieving not one loss, but a lifestyle of ongoing losses. When the powerful move in to execute the kill, it is as if a giant monster reaches into the life of any one of us and ruthlessly plucks a prized possession, a dream, an achievement, or anything of value in an insidious, ongoing, institutionalized assault. Legalized injustice attacks deep convictions that idealistically guide good people toward decent decisions. Disillusioned victims state that such losses annihilate the cherished beliefs that make up the essence of their beings - an amputation of their spirits.

There never is a time that spiritual strength is more important than during the grieving process. Loss seems to cue us into our need for a greater perception of life. The walking wounded who suffer LAS are often deprived of an easy reliance on the spiritual because the pain has reached so deeply into the core of their existence. John Bradshaw, in *The Family*, refers to "soul murder," describing those whose pain and suffering prevents them from being all that they could have been in life. The pain that one must endure when trust is violated leaves the victim often unable to trust that a God exists or, at least, that a loving God exists.

That fact must be acknowledged. A supportive listener might ask, "I'm wondering if it feels like God has abandoned you?" or "When the moral code is broken down to this extent, do you find it hard to identify the first step, the guiding sense out of the pain?" Patients have responded well to the idea that within them is a spiritual flow or component that is part of every personality. Even though we're numbed at the moment, it is there, and with time, patience, and exploration, a path will emerge. That path may or may not connect victims with a God or Supreme Being, but a spiritual path is there. Organized religion sometimes has little to do with the person's ability to have a rich spiritual existence and to gain comfort from openness to a spiritual reservoir.

When we can tap into our spiritual strength, regardless of our beliefs, we can reframe the losses into a purge, leaving a void. How that void is filled again becomes our new journey. It starts with the debriefing process and the acknowledgment of just what was lost. Although sometimes through embarrassment, the victim must admit painful losses that may not, on the surface, seem worthy of mention. Underlying these tangible losses are usually profound intangible losses.

Aforementioned losses have included:

1. Losses of those who felt like friends but didn't remain friends after money was lost.
   Intangible losses - social identity, trust, belief system.

2. Loss of a gold card and the status that went with it.
   Intangible losses—business identity, earned credit status.

3. Loss of a wet bar and the way it was the center of social interaction.
   Intangible losses - sense of providing fun and closeness.

4. Loss of ability to pay for children's music lessons.
   Intangible losses - earned life style and expectation of self as parent.

5. Loss of a pet.
   Intangible losses - warmth, trust, and companionship.

It is okay to grieve over personal, ridiculous-appearing losses as well as the big ones. The person has pain and it is okay to grieve that pain to the extent to which it is felt. What the loss meant to you is what counts. There is no way to qualify and no advantage to placing limits on the pain and anguish a victim feels. The depth of the cumulative losses can reach to the soul even if the first tear is shed over a gerbil. Certainly there is no scale that can weigh or no continuum upon which one person can assess the degree of another person's pain after loss. Again, as in debriefing, it is important to accept the significance of the loss to the victim. Victims need to be embraced by sensitivity regardless of the rationality of the loss. Feelings exist without rationale. Grief will heal best in a milieu of respect, as part of the victim experience. Victims need to be given a wide berth with no moral or value judgement.

We cannot prepare so as to avoid the total trauma of loss even if it is anticipated or threatened. We can help to prevent some of the shock stage, however. Stark meanness and callous legal flogging are unexpected by the victim. Rehearsal which includes bracing for the anticipated assaults promotes emotional readiness. The following principles offer a guideline for self-talk of LAS victims:

Operational Principles for Acceptance of Self in Grief

> **REALIZATION** - I realize that I am suffering the most profound loss known to man, loss of trust.
>
> **PERMISSION TO SHED TEARS OVER TIERS** of trauma - It's okay to cry over tangible losses; they usually relate to significant intangible losses.
>
> **PREPARATION** - If litigation or courts are part of my victimization, I must prepare for brutal realities of the system so I can prevent the shock stage of grief.
>
> **CONSTRICTION vs ISOLATION** - My life will be narrowed by mental censorship and avoidance

of painful memories and thoughts. I won't let constriction turn to isolation.

PATIENCE AND CONSOLATION - Silent sobbing in my core is my lonely secret. I will be patient with my progress and pain and will console, not criticize, myself.

Chapter 5

Obsession

The Heart of Accomplishment

> *Friends and advisors will tell the victim,*
> *"You can't let yourself be obsessed by this,"*
> *"It is all you think about, " and*
> *"Put it behind you."*

In fact, the victim cannot *not* be obsessed. Figuring out what happened and forming a basis for feeling safe again preoccupies the victim's life. What defines a critical traumatic incident is the degree of helplessness or lack of control that was felt at the time it happened. Every LAS survivor has been in jeopardy and absolutely unable to do <u>anything</u> about <u>something</u>. That something, in the face of his or her impotence, will trigger fear motivating obsession[1].

People do not choose their reactions to a traumatic assault. Their responses will be "knee-jerk" reactions that reflect the person's orientation to relationships and life events. Bev Flanigan outlines three examples which are helpful in identifying certain obsessive styles.

   1. "Pilot-in-command"- This person is the master of his habitat. His control relies on the assumption that others will be somewhat predictable in their reactions to him or her. When that trust is violated,

---

[1] An obsession is a persistent idea or thought which the individual recognizes as irrational but cannot seem to ignore. A compulsion is an act that is performed even though the person knows it is irrational and may even choose not to do it. For the purpose of this work, the word obsession encompasses obsessive and compulsive acts. Patients report that obsession

he must quickly try to restructure his belief system. Obsession revolves around the question, "How can I bring things back into control?" The question is urgent to the pilot in command because he has never faced his vulnerability. This type of controller can be brought to his knees by one event. Businesspeople are often of this orientation. They've functioned as the pilot of enterprises fostering predictable behaviors from family, employees, and the business community. Suddenly, the "pilot is grounded" due to no fault of his own.

2. "Dependent" - The dependent type of orientation causes one to feel that others are in control. This type of person needs protection. Every relationship is set up for the purpose of satisfying dependency needs. There is a strong assumption that the system functions to help in time of need. Deceptive crimes followed by betrayal by the system cause a critical loss of faith in life itself.

3. "Mathematician" - Recovery for this type of person is the toughest. His obsession forms around the question, "What are the rules?" Rules guide everything. He listens for formulas. Examples are "God protects us if we are good," and "If something bad happens to me, I must be getting paid back for something I did in the past." The therapist or helper must force clear identification of rules that

---

is the word that most precisely communicates this phase of post traumatic stress. The obsessive phase is marked more by thoughts than acts. Commonly, the LAS victim acts normally while being tortured by painful, obsessive thoughts.

have failed the victim. Otherwise, this type of individual will obsess around forming a new set of commandments.

My experience with victims struggling with obsessions have produced the following additional types:

1. Anti-dependent - This individual goes far beyond independence, to "I don't need anyone for anything," and "To Hell with the whole world." These statements characterize the anti-dependent person in times of stress. The danger in being anti-dependent emerges when the victim needs advice or help and he or she has shut out the world. Imminent consequences do not motivate this type of person to accept help from others. Whatever the price of anti-dependence, it does not seem as menacing to the victim as mingling with the world.

2. Indecisive - This type of obsession leaves the person unable to feel comfortable with decisions - even to the point of driving between locations unable to decide which place to go, if anyplace. They will go shopping and come home with nothing.

3. Figuring it out - The person spends most waking moments and many asleep trying to figure out why the deception happened or trying to make it fit

some logical schema. It feels like finding a reason for the occurrence might make it all right.

4. Inventorying - Counting money or belongings, and worrying they all won't be there, consumes the inventorier. The victim perceives that everything is disposable. There is an overwhelming sensation that, at any time, anything might randomly disappear.

5. Control of the uncontrollable - Having to get the mail on time and being the one to get the mail first are good examples of trying to control the uncontrollable. These people expend extraordinary amounts of energy in an attempt to control regular eventualities.

6. Security guard - The security guard is never going to get "duped" again. He spends his life checking and rechecking windows, doors, locks, receipts, or the locations of valuables and often carries mace and other weapons.

7. Hoarding - The hoarder stores things, worries about scarcity, hides a stash of money, paperwork, food, alcohol or anything he values.

Legal Abuse Syndrome

8. Night terror - Nightly rituals characterize the night terror types. Daunted by nighttime, they struggle to cope. All-out efforts are mobilized to contend with fear of going to sleep or not going to sleep. They're rapt with meanings of nightmares and impending dreams or sleepless nights.

9. Lifeguard - Health is the obsession for the lifeguard. Status checks on family members, trips to the doctor, and taking pets to the veterinarian are common. A sense of well being is never felt.

10. Revenge - Immersion in recompense drowns this type. He feels life can't go on until he gets even. It is important to help this person realize that revenge is strictly for fantasy. It backfires on decent people when carried out in reality.

11. "World Sucks" - The awful preoccupies the mind. If there is negativity, "World Sucks" will find it. If there isn't, he'll perceive it. It's hard to have a good time with "World Sucks" types. It's hard to be around or to be motivated to help them.

12. Mt. Everest climbers - Exhaustion greets every task. If there is a chore, Mt. Everest must be climbed before the chore is efficiently completed. These are truly the sick and tired, the walking wounded.

13. Perfect Sufferer - From an idealistic stance this individual can submit, in detail, that he was right at all times. Being right, doing the right thing, and all it should have bought the victim, has been violated. He is consumed by the fact that "wrong" won. This person suffers a great deal of anxiety as his obsession spirals. The victim is indignant due to the inversion of his belief system about justice and fairness as the reward of the righteous. This type will be defensive and able to list every wrong the other side committed.

Judy's Bout with Obsession

Judy was a dependent type in terms of her orientation to life, even though, to look at her, she would appear independent. After finding that her money and her husband had fled together, she could no longer deny that she had married a criminal. The criminal's final letter to her advised her to change her name and leave town. Feelings of terror struck. She had no idea from whom he had stolen or how they might strike back. Judy's automatic response was to reach out for someone to protect her. Dependence can be dangerous when the victim is reaching from a point of vulnerability. Her dependent style backfired on her as she counted on people to fit her image as her protectors. The myriad others involved in the fallout of this deception included creditors, her husband's "business associates," the FBI, the criminal investigation division of the IRS, and "vultures" ready to buy her things for 10 cents on the dollar. No one offered rescue.

Judy's case shows how peril from every direction was part of the aftermath of her abandonment. Agencies, bureaucracies, organizations, all in the courses of their various duties, inadvertently added assault to injury. There were legalized takers[2]. She turned to an attorney to separate her legally from the mess. The attorney inquired as to the funds she had left and promptly absorbed them as his retainer. She was broke when the attorney informed her in court that it would cost another $1450 to have him accomplish the annulment that she had retained him to do. Judy describes leaving the courthouse in a daze. The lawyer that she depended upon had joined her husband in perpetration of profound and unforgivable deceit. Obsessions began to emerge.

Everyday, Judy rendezvoused with the mailperson, not by choice. Her "husband" had always beat her to the mail. That mail became a focal point of Judy losing control. Today, she still has an obsession about getting the mail. She goes into a state of anxiety if the mailperson is late in delivery of the mail or if anyone else gets the mail from the box.

---

[2] Taking has to do with power differential. The powerful take from the less powerful. A taking can be legal or it can be illegal. The IRS, FBI or DEA can take property and money. Takings open the door for obscure theft. When one party has the power and opportunity to take what belongs to others, it challenges what American citizenship is all about. Takers

Another obsession that kicked in at an inopportune time was the grocery-packing obsession. She avoids carrying her groceries into the house. Somehow, because her husband used to walk behind her as they carried in groceries, she cannot turn the corner on the sidewalk while carrying groceries without the feeling that he is behind her. So, she arranges the groceries to be carried in by someone else.

Not much dust had settled when Judy was served with papers from a former "business associate" and best man at her wedding. He had filed suit to take her house; a new attempt at an illegal taking was beginning.

Obsession saps energy and complicates one's ability to regain a sense of control of life. The FBI and the IRS are powerful entities. When they intend to take, however legally, the process seems to challenge an individual's basic rights and freedoms to the core. They advise the victim of due process. If the victim is to exercise due process at a critical moment, it requires the person to be alert and able to clearly respond to charges. Their memories need to be intact and they must have energy and money in order to focus on effective defense. A mega-dose of helplessness followed by chicanery make fair due process impossible for the LAS victim.

While Judy is using her energy to meet the mailperson and get the neighbor kids, adults, passers-by, or mailperson to carry in her groceries, she is set up for a sleazy taking. Then her house and assets were threatened by a legal taking. The IRS began an audit on her

---

often use their positions of power or trust to steal. Then, they try to conceal the reality of what they have done in "procedure," paperwork, or omission. These thieves attack while the trail of pain is still hot.

fugitive husband's taxes. They advised her that, if she could not pay taxes that they deemed were owed, they could take any property, income, or bank accounts that she had. Of course, they advised her that she could use due process procedures. She describes that her eyes were so swollen from crying they couldn't even read the fine print on the documents, let alone was she in any state of being to mount a self-defense. The metaphor "David and Goliath" has been used to communicate imbalances of power. The chapters on empowerment and reframing will present a different viewpoint on power differential.

Like an automaton, she continued to sell things, anything. Functioning like a machine, she parted with treasured items. Her jewelry, her piano, her furnishings, clothing, gifts, appliances, or anything that anyone would buy was sold. She fed her kids, paid basic bills, and had to pay another attorney to try to protect her house.

Obsession presents an emotional hyperbole that exhausts the LAS victim. It is like containing a raging bull in your chest as you attend to the day's demands. The victim has a window of energy early in the day and finds the evenings a time of total wipe-out. Sleep may come early, but a troubled twilight sleep will usually greet the victim at dawn. It is a time that leaves the victim asking, "What's wrong with me?" and saying, "I've gone completely nuts."

What to do About Obsession

- Name it
- Face it
- Own it
- Accept it
- Manage it

Name It (or Them)

Look at the styles described previously. Any combination might make up your obsessive style. You may need to create new ones as well. Once you can name your obsessive style, the first step toward mastery has been taken. James was a combination of "Mt. Everest"/ "Perfect Sufferer"/"Revenge" and had moments of "World sucks."

Face It

A sense of humor is a principle asset when dealing with obsession. The ability to laugh at oneself and with others relieves anxiety and lends to self acceptance. All victims do weird things after being assaulted. I have seen people suffering loss of their children due to court battles, facing possible incarceration, and victims who've sustained profound ruin. We shared obsessions, owned up to strange behaviors, and we have laughed until tears rolled down our cheeks. Facing our obsessions is a coming out.

Judy's sense of humor was a savior. She became a decent negotiator. She didn't feel as crazy after naming and describing her obsessions in an accepting group. A deep concern that she had perverse secrets to be hidden from the world was eased. In spite of her predicament, she was able to laugh at herself and the pure ridiculousness of the situation. Judy became more independent and, rather than expecting others to protect her, protected herself. Some good news followed. The new attorney took reasonable payments and saved her house. The IRS agent listened to her story, checked everything out, and gave her time to recover. She is left with the knowledge, however, that someday she will have to pay the nonperson's taxes. At least the IRS agent was not instituting a taking on her at that time.

Own It

Your combination of obsessive behaviors are uniquely yours. Rarely do obsessions manifest themselves exactly alike among people. It isn't so tough to own what you have straightforwardly reconciled. Until you grab the obsession and own it, it will grab and own you.

Accept It

Accept the obsession as a natural part of the response process. Don't fight it or feel guilty about it. Resisting or succumbing in secret to the obsessions intensifies them. They are there as a healthy and natural reaction to a devastating circumstance. There is a gentle way out.

Manage It

Re-look at "what I can control" from the list previously generated. Expand it if necessary. To right the wrongs, create goals designed to empower some action. Actions can be direct or indirect. James and John chose direct pro se actions. P.J. supports organizations that are advocating victim's needs.

Compartmentalization of time is the main component of management of LAS obsession. Setting aside a time period with a beginning and an end is the first task. It is a promise to oneself that certain hours of the week will be spent on empowerment in the areas where control has been lost. In other words, the victim schedules his way out of obsession. Compartmentalization helps in the following ways:

1. It validates the victim's need to own and deal with the issues that cause fear and loss of control.

2. Well-planned activities are more productive than non directed, obsessive, and intrusive thoughts.

3. Completion of empowering activities relieves the intensity of the obsessive feelings.

4. It substitutes for revenge and bitterness and prevents an obsessive spiral producing sardonic, disillusioned people.

James and John both have taken their legal battles onward as pro se, meaning without an attorney. Designating time each week to spend on their cases empowers them to continue the fight. Otherwise, outrage spills into every waking hour at random. Groundwork must be laid for facing the traumatic issues in compartments or increments. James calls it "jumping into the sewer" for a few hours each week. He has to emotionally prepare himself for tasks that will be frustrating. Those who enter court pro se find the deck is loaded against them. They will be vilified, dismissed, and thwarted. James dealt with all of the following during his weekly compartmentalized times.

> James noticed that his file in the Bankruptcy Court clerk's office had been altered. He decided that before any more legal work was to be done, he would have his entire file copied and marked in the presence of witnesses. They would then sign a notarized document in order to protect himself against further tampering.
>
> It was expensive but he ordered his file. The clerk brought one small file to him. He responded that it had to be larger than that. Then, the clerk brought two more files and insisted that those 600 pages were the entire file in three sections. He ordered them copied.
>
> On the day they were to be picked up, he called the court and found that three more files were still on the shelf and had been overlooked completely. James insisted that they be copied also. He was admonished since he was not there to fill out the form. The file would have to be requested by the copyperson and would cost $10.00 (in addition to copying costs). They were copied. Then more files were found under the name of the criminal contractor who'd caused James the problem from the start.
>
> No explanation was ever given as to why James' file would be filed under his adversary's name.

Those files were copied. Before he was done, eight more files turned up after he had informed them that he would file a motion for production of the documents. Total cost for copying his files came to $312.00. This was added to $8,000. for obtaining his transcript from a hearing. These files are the foundation of pro se work. Sadly, resistance from every turn and substantial expense are involved for the *pro se*. However, when faced in two-hour segments, James was prepared and effectively managed his obsessions.

Hardly earth-shattering, but viciously frustrating, are the routine acts of incompetence, blasé and even rude behaviors committed by the employees who work for the taxpayers. It further complicates victims' abilities to continue a fight. James' mouth goes dry, his heart pounds, his blood pressure elevates, and flashbacks consume his senses when he enters the Federal Court Building. It was the site where his emotional blood was shed as the product of his life's work was taken from him.

He has to force composure past an hyper-obsessive urge to blow the place up. James reminds himself that only for the scheduled hours will he be "slimed." He has received support through networking, use of paralegals, and help from victims. James has victims at the other ends of phones, nationwide. They stand by for one another when the path gets tough.

Chapter 6

Blaming
The Responsibility of the Victim

<u>Only</u> *by identifying the wrongdoer and confronting evil in moral terms, justice is felt.*
<u>Only</u> *when justice is felt will the wrongdoer be accepted again into society.*
<u>Only</u> *when justice is felt will the victim truly recover.*
(Anonymous victim)

Undeserved pain and suffering is an intolerable idea whether one is of the twentieth century or was a primitive being. Those with shattered lives and all who witness injustice will grasp for a reason. Throughout history, rituals to neutralize evil forces have been developed. Bargaining with evil forces, at the extreme, has seen animal and human sacrifices. Diverse superhuman justifications are offered to the suffering to explain untoward life events. Victims have reached into past lives as well as looked forward as they hoped for justice through Karma wherein the future metes out the rewards and punishments for good and evil acts. Good versus evil behaviors are classically cited as forces that shape one's destiny. A master force sitting in omnipresence determines what is good or bad. Unless the censure or punishment is relegated to Karma or the spiritual, blaming is a healing responsibility.

Blaming, the First Step Toward Justice

Who is to blame when a deceptive crime is committed? Someone to blame and/or something to attribute the act to is part of the struggle for the victim to manage and regain some sense of safety and security. Attribution is part of the eternal struggle to come to terms with evil.

Retribution is the natural balancing factor after an assault. There was once the "golden age of the victim," around the beginning of the middle ages. The victim's role was to rise up, take his friends and family members, and "get even." The "blood feud" was often the manner in which, by whatever means, the victims extracted recompense from the victor.

Old English tradition, which our court system is patterned after, believes that justice is best served when the defendant and the state clash over the crime. No one would argue that civilization requires that we give up blood feud's violent vengeance. However, the settling of scores has evolved in a manner that prevents natural closure to the victim/victor experience because they're relinquished to the criminal justice system.

All functional and equalizing responsibilities of the criminal and victim, as participants in society, have dissipated. The victim has not only been left ignored, he is usually viciously, verbally attacked, wrongfully blamed in the court, and stigmatized by society. There is a simple expectation. Courts exist to punish the wrong and reward the right. If that expectation is violated, there remains neither means for the criminal to be brought back into the fold, nor for the victim to be rewarded for doing right.

Society benefits by adhering to the ultimate goal of sanctioning the good and providing restitution for the victim, and both punishment and rehabilitation for the criminal. However, victims are suffering from the influences of Menninger and other social scientists of the 1960's who espoused the idea of "deprisonizing" the justice system. The New York School of Social Work and Columbia University produced work which claimed that punishing people for committing crimes did not work (Wilson). They recommended rehabilitation, alternate sentencing, and community-based corrections. The focus was on social ills and the mental health of the criminal. Much of this occurred during the Johnson Administration.

Intrinsic "rightness" and "wrongness" was sacrificed to the "deviance theory" during the 60's. Howard Becker, one of the leading deviance theorists, put forth that all social rules and morality are essentially relative. The spotlight was turned on the people who made the rules and who would, therefore, condemn the actions of others. All actions were to be judged by varying rules. Since rulemakers are inherently favorable to themselves, the rules were in question. Those who made the rules were said to "label" others who didn't. According to this theory, crime was not seen as bad in itself. Instead, it related to the label or judgment imposed on another by an elite group of rulemakers. Throughout this period, inadvertently, loser and cry-baby images of victims began slowly to develop like a Polaroid picture. Many crimes faded into invisibility, and blame became distasteful.

Guilt, The Hidden Monster, Looms Again

Floating, unconscious guilt is an undetected monster within the hearts of LAS victims. Victims don't report guilt; they describe a feeling of punishment, in fact, "cruel and unusual punishment." However, guilt, denied by the victim, often is part of the picture. Guilt must be dealt with or it will lie within, quietly ravaging the victim for a lifetime.

Victims experience guilt when betrayed because:

1. They relinquished control of their lives.
2. Their families and others have also been hurt by invisible assaults.
3. Shame fills the core of the hostage, even if the hostage-taker is clearly in the wrong, because ***right and wrong do not determine the degree of guilt suffered by the LAS victim. Loss of control of one's life is the most profound precipitator of guilt and shame.***

Therapists and helpers must plunge through the denial in pursuit of the guilt. It then can be put to logical terms. What does guilt look like? How does guilt feel? Victims in denial will argue that they do not feel guilty, just angry. When questioned further, patients reveal that they are angry at themselves. The person will persist with anger or rage when, in fact, guilt is at the bottom of it all. It is an embittering force. Behaviors that signal guilt are:

1. Distrust
2. Shame
3. Rage
4. Terror
5. Grief
6. Suicide ideation
7. Homicide ideation
8. Hatred
9. Withdrawal
10. Defensiveness

Self-destructive behaviors unquestionably relate to guilt. It is important to emphasize that for LAS survivors, their guilt is undeserved and displaced. Guilt, rage, anger, and wrong all need to be directed where they belong, at the offender. The purpose is to achieve the first step toward healthy blame. Until it is put where it is deserved, through relevant blaming, the job of recovery will be left wanting.

Removing Barriers to Blame

Let's look at some facts about criminals and illicit acts from a societal panorama. Bringing this type of information to the victim is helpful in putting guilt into perspective. Firstly, criminals are defined by their behaviors, nothing else. Explicitly, these are behaviors freely chosen which victimize other people and deprive them of their basic rights. Crime is not caused by anything identifiable; it is a life-style of persistently neglecting the rights of other individuals.

Deceptive crimes are crimes of perception. Criminals have pessimistic motives. Cynical attitude becomes a justification to betray others. Criminals rationalize and twist the viewpoints of the authorities and can appear sincere from their angelic stances. Therefore, deceptive crimes become burdensome for law enforcement to evaluate. Every deception is further affected by distortion, varying insights, paradigms, and prejudices that alter the ways in which an invisible crime is perceived. Therefore, LAS victims don't receive clear and consistent responses to their assaults.

Furthering the dilemma of the conscience-centered person[3], who approaches the "system" expecting it to be a solver of such

---

[3] Conscience-centered people are motivated by their consciences. Their behaviors reflect a strong commitment to doing what they deem right vs wrong. Power-centered people are motivated by need for power regardless of prudence or propriety. These concepts are further explored in the chapter on "Deshaming."

crime, is the fact that the power-centered person intends to deceive. He will manipulate and play on the biases, imaginations, errors, and confusion throughout the legal and regulatory systems. Corporations are perfect examples.

Corporations have become major creators of LAS victims. They would not call their assaults criminal, however. Corporations are business entities who function in a capitalistic manner. They do not possess feelings or consciences, as people do. They do have money, teams of attorneys, and lobbyists. Corporations have power without virtue. Since the operations of corporations are carried out by many people, with varying belief systems, and the "bottom line" is the goal, behaviors will not adhere to a singular moral and ethical code. When an individual is assaulted by corporate behavior, shame is only felt by the victim. In a court battle, cold, calculated strategy repeatedly strikes the victim. If guilt is felt, it is the property of the victim alone (Greider).

Legalized interpretations of right and wrong have skewed the issues of blame, morality, crime, and good and bad to the extent that there is no meaningful avenue for wrong to be righted in our society. Legal versus illegal trickery does not adequately substitute for right and wrong. LAS victims are left struggling, trusting no one, and searching for the missing measure for human behavior. Moral turpitude, couched in legalese and official trappings, and presented by Presidents and judges, leaves the victim unable to distinctly define "who did what to whom." Blame becomes a hovering blimp casting shadows over many but never landing on a definitive target. Thus, closure for victims is foiled.

It's a Dirty Job and Nobody's Doing It

The complexity of communication regarding deceptive crime is immense. LAS litigants find themselves at regulators' offices or in court with all of the components of an effective case. They have evidence. They are postured to win. They are purportedly represented by an institution that stands for justice. Then they are neutralized. Bureaucracy, intervening steps and delays, multiple statutes and loopholes, offenders' "Constitutional rights," self deception, and sleight of hand culminate to offer the pièce de résistance to the dishonest bureaucrat, attorney, or judge. None, in the end, has a personal motive to stay in the fight. Only the offended is motivated to take on the dirty job of blaming. Others are rarely inspired in LAS cases to "get involved" in the blaming phase and see it through. If systems help too little, then what path is left for the citizen with character, integrity, and honor? The natural path of blaming is denied to the victim.

Three Click-Whirr (automatic) Blame Styles

As is true of obsessive and grieving responses to victimization, style of blaming is not a conscious choice made by the victim. It is a spontaneous and a dynamic process. The victim struggles to cope with his disorganized life by an automatic mustering of forces. Helping the victim to understand the process and the style he is manifesting helps bring a sense of awareness and self-governing, alleviating further crises.

Self-Blame
I Did It—Somehow, Someway it is Ultimately My Fault

A prevailing myth provides that the victim asks for his assault. Self-blame is convenient and will be quickly affirmed by the observer's need to attribute the crime. If victims are responsible for their own plight, then we are not responsible to help them. Blaming oneself feels courageous and responsible and, also, tricks the mind into believing that if self is to blame, the self then can fix the problem.

Self-Blame Checklist

Check the statements that describe how you feel about your victimization.

1. _____ I feel responsible.
2. _____ I took a chance and shouldn't have.
3. _____ It happened because I've done wrong in the past.
4. _____ I should have seen it coming.
5. _____ I was stupid.
6. _____ If I just hadn't.......
7. _____ It was an expensive education.
8. _____ How can I be so gullible?
9. _____ I got what I deserved.
10. _____ I knew better.
11. _____ I've hurt so many people.
12. _____ I wish I had it to do over again.

Self-Blame Complications

Those people who are conscience-centered are especially prone to self-blame. Here is where codependent [4] overlays complicate the recovery process. The codependent person accepts responsibility too quickly for the wrongdoing and spends energy searching to understand the crime from the criminal's point of view by saying, "Maybe he came from poverty," "Maybe he was a victim of society," or "Maybe he needed whatever he stole to feed a starving family or a wounded ego." It may sound compassionate, but it is abuse of self.

Self-blame is dangerous. Therapists and friends must intervene because self-blame will cause the victim to look guilty. When a person exudes guilt, he or she will act in ways that draw suspicion. It is important to shape the experience to reveal the fact, to the victim, that he feels and looks guilty because he or she has been forced to surrender responsibility, and not because he has done wrong (Bard, Sangrey).

Difficulties caused by self-blame:

1. Self-blame can be turned on litigants in court by clever defense attorneys, forcing them to admit some unconscious complicity or create that image.

2. Police officers or prosecutors who sense this guilt might view the victim with suspicion. The entire crime can be misperceived by the guilty appearance of the innocent.

---

[4] Codependency is a term that describes behaviors of those who have learned to respond to others' needs rather than to act in their own behalves. It is a disorder of priorities in relationships.

3. Self-blame can cause those around the victim to hold back supportive behavior and even to make remarks that demean the victim or otherwise mirror the self-blame.

4. Self-blame removes the victim from being entitled to restitution, community resources, and comfort.

5. Self-blame lets the criminal off the hook. It perpetuates and reinforces the criminal behavior.

Another mode of blame comes in a broad form called "they" blame. "They" blame, blames nebulous forces.

NOT CLEAR

They Did It
If Not for "Them," It Would Not Have Happened
Examples of "they":

- Divorce rate
- Failures of churches and schools
- State of modern medicine
- Corrupt politicians
- Permissiveness
- Offender protected society

Difficulties caused by "They" blame:

1. "They" blame allows the victim full entitlement to feel righteously angry without learning from the experience.

2. Sense of hopelessness increases because the target is so large and unclear that there is little the victim can do to effect it.

3. The victim may become accusatory with law enforcement officers or court personnel, and alienate those from whom he needs help.

4. The victim's support system, family, and friends, can be put on the defensive by other blaming remarks and, therefore, not be there to help the victim.

5. "They" blaming can cause further personal crises if, for example, blame of a spouse or a business partner creates an additional crisis in a relationship.

A compelling need to get even dictates the third blaming style:

I Know Exactly Who Did It
"An Eye for an Eye" Revenge

Acts of revenge bring momentary pleasure. It is punishment, of sorts, where the victim's will is exercised to the disadvantage of the perpetrator. Drawbacks to revenge are found in the facts that:

1. Immediate, impulsive counterattack may attack the wrong person or entity on insufficient evidence.

2. Well planned and successfully executed revenge takes tremendous amounts of time and energy. When compared with appropriate blaming actions, the risk often outweighs the rewards.

3. It may violate the values of the victim. Eventually it brings more shame and guilt. "How can I be so mean?," clients will ask, shocked at their ability to avenge.

4. Revenge, taken too far, destroys the conscience-centered person's self-esteem. They fear that they are becoming corrupt. They've violated their own standards.

5. It magnifies flaws when we're working to recover self-image.

6. If revenge moves accelerate on both sides, they will tend to be accelerated symmetrically (Flanigan). It may be a war wherein retaliation becomes the focus.

Revenge is great in fantasy, however. Revengeful thoughts are not to be worried about as long as they are fleeting contemplations. Their help in provoking creative thinking assists in finding the most appropriate blaming processes.

Who Gets the Blame?

Who violated the moral contract? Could the violator have foreseen the pain he was causing? Did the violator know in advance that the victim would be injured as a result of his actions? Bev Flanigan, in *Forgiving the Unforgivable*, gives a list of qualifiers as they relate to intimate injuries:

1. Justifiability - Was the violator coerced in any way that might justify the assault?

2. Intentionality - Was it intended? Were the results known and the decision to hurt the other planned? This evil intent weighs the scale dramatically toward blame.

3. Foreseeability - Could the violator have foreseen the pain that would follow?

4. Cause - Did it happen to me because of just being there, or was I the target?

5. Association - Was a relationship of trust violated by this action?

Violation of the Moral Code as a Basis for Assigning Blame

But in spite of all possible points of view everyone will admit that there are crimes which always and everywhere from the beginning of the world, under all legal systems, have unhesitatingly been considered crimes and will be considered so as long as man remains human, said Dostoevski (Tucker).

First and foremost, the moral code addresses abuse of power. Regardless of legalese, victims want to blame those who violate the heart and all codes and commitments that were set forth to guide human behavior. All humans agree that the guidelines, in some way, provide that: (1) I may not violate your right to live and enjoy what you have earned, (2) you may live in a climate of freedom, to think and function as you wish, and (3) your actions will not violate my right to live and enjoy what is mine and to think and function according to my conscience. If a violation occurs, then I have the right to confront you and inform you that you have violated the moral contract. All justice systems are designed and obligated to stand for and enforce that code.

The act of blaming requires that the victim look deeply within his own values. Victims must ask themselves, "What do I really want to happen as a result of blaming?" Some victims are satisfied if the violator is never able to assault another again. Some want restitution. Some will settle for the violator's punishment. The victim confronting the blamed is the first step toward rebuilding trust. We have ascertained that loss of trust is the greatest loss known to man. Deception and willful destruction of trust is a transgression recognized by every victim. Since society cannot sustain itself without trust, blaming becomes a social responsibility.

Fritz Heider calls it the "filtering process" when one establishes who is to be blamed for what and then what is to be done with the offender (Shaver). Normally, there are many offenders of varying dimensions mixed into the assaults of the LAS victim. Degrees of blame are assessed accordingly (see Figure 5). Then a blaming action is selected.

After the degree of blame is assigned to the various violators, a blaming action can be instituted. The degree refers to the amount of personal investment in blaming that is appropriately assumed by the victim. If the violator intended to hurt the victim personally, and could have foreseen the pain his actions would cause, it is a personal blaming issue for the victim. If a corporation rip-off occurred, the violator is harder to personally identify and blame. More impersonal blaming actions are chosen in those cases.

Categories for Assessing Blame

Blaming actions will either be personal or generic. Personal actions require the offended to take personal responsibility for initiating a blaming action. The best personal blaming actions are achieved when the victim is allowed to have an eyeball-to-eyeball, heart-to-heart encounter with the offender to inform the offender of the violation of the moral code. Profoundly effective are personal confrontations resulting in sincere apologies, changes in behaviors, and restitution for the victims. The following graphic outlines a system for establishing the degree of blaming action to institute.

Violations of the Moral Code

Degrees of Blame

Perpetrator's
Violation   Blaming Action

1st DEGREE BLAME

Violates Trust Personal/Institutional
Intended to Cause Suffering
Foreseeable
Initiated Assault
Charades/Court

2nd DEGREE BLAME

System Joined Violator
Part of group that Violates
Actions Destructive to Societal Good
"Hired guns"

3rd DEGREE BLAME*

Forced to violate
Non-intentional
Quits When Aware of Violation
Part of Job or Contract

*Example of 3rd Degree - eviction by manager

Figure 5 - Violations of the Moral Code

If the blaming action is effective in causing the offender to genuinely realize the moral law that was broken and to apologize, make restitution, and actively do what is agreed upon as right, recovery may occur after the blaming stage. Indeed, if the blaming action causes justice to occur, such as the court process working as it was intended, recovery is imminent.

MADD (Mothers Against Drunk Drivers) has instituted victim impact panels. The survivors and victims of drunk drivers confront the offenders in exactly the manner prescribed above. It has been effective in promoting victims' and survivors' recoveries. Change in behavior and attitude of the drunk driver is a major factor in the victim sensing that justice has been accomplished. How many times do we hear victims of horrific assaults say that they have gone public simply to try to prevent the victimization of any more people? Societal correction is at the heart of a victim's need to blame.

Blaming Actions

Blaming actions need to be approached like a think tank activity. No quick evaluation should extinguish any suggestion, no matter how outrageous it may seem. A volume of actions need to be generated first and then evaluated later. Blaming actions that work may be surprising. Some of the most effective have been used by creative judges who adjudicate the labeling of convicted persons. Drunk drivers in Texas were forced to use a bumper sticker that identified them as convicted drunk drivers. A child molester was forced to place a sign stating such in his front yard. These were extremely therapeutic for the offended. It seems to satisfy the protective need to publicize in order to keep others from harm.

A blaming action must bring satisfaction to the victim in order to be considered effective. Traditional blaming actions are usually lawsuits, complaints to regulators and consumer groups, and reporting to Congresspeople. LAS victims find these channels have become so bogged down in bureaucratic ritual that there is rarely satisfaction to be obtained by their use. Even when the victim prevails in court, money awards, even large awards, in and of themselves, have not been comforting results of the blaming actions. Often the money award is never paid due to appeals and legal gameplaying and, even if it is paid, it seems that money helps but does not satisfy the need for restoration of the moral code. Therefore, no system in place effectively rights the wrong and restores the victim.

Mediation and arbitration, conducted by a thorough and fair referee, show promise as long as the actions have an empowering effect on the victim. In cases where there has been profound violation of the moral code, the victim will not feel a sense of closure if a referee "smooths over" rather than takes a stand in behalf of right and responsibility. Again, the victim will not feel appeased if there is no genuine repentance on the part of the wrongdoer. The moral code cannot be mediated out.

If the blaming action produces a false apology, patronization of the moral code, and false promises with no intention of complying with moral law, it prevents satisfaction in the victim. As in the cases of LAS, the offender and the "system" or the protector become one and the same. Unfinished business gnaws at the victim. If, as in James' court cases, the entity issues no apology, no promise, and no concern and further attacks the victim as a means of defense or strategy to begin recovery, all eight steps outlined in this book are required. Otherwise, restoration is denied and recovery becomes tenuous.

Punishment, an Incomplete Process

Punishment is directly tied to power. The wrongdoer exerted power over the victim. Punishment allows the victim or his representatives to strip that power from the criminal and to apply a counteracting power.

Society punishes criminals in order to separate them from the population as a whole, restrain their criminal activities, and to set an example in order to prevent others from committing crimes. Groups usually remove privileges, ostracize, yell at, condemn, and censure wrong behaviors.

All human societies and organizations use punishment of some sort. Restitution is a part of the punishment picture. However, punishment fails to target the moral violation and to consistently change future behavior.

The Task of Blaming

> James first blamed and sued the contractor. The contractor was blamed to the first degree. Second degree blame was assessed to the bank and the trustee. The bank was sued and the trustee is being sued *pro se*. Third degree blame came to rest on the attorneys, who advised the bank, the contractor and the trustee. They were wrong, but did not set out to hurt James independently of their clients.

Suing the contractor was an appropriate blaming action. However, in James' case, the system joined with the criminal in a bankruptcy scam. It wasn't until eight years had passed that the scam was made public (Appendix C).

> James reported, "It would be more gratifying to see the bankruptcy court have to post a sign on every location and a sticker on every document: **'WARNING: BANKRUPTCY COURT MAY BE INJURIOUS TO YOUR HEALTH AND EVEN FATAL IF ENTERED WITH ASSETS.'"**

To what degree do I have a right or responsibility to blame and punish?

> James had dozens of people who had participated in his demise. James' click-whirr response was to blame himself. His actions became defensive. It was during this time that his wife describes him as suffering from acute "asshole." He was not likeable. No one was sympathetic and the more they reacted to his defensiveness, the more he blamed himself. Guilt overwhelmed him concerning the suffering his decisions had caused his family. But, he was unable to say so.
>
> James had to look at his debriefing sheet and name the offenders. Then he had to face who made the decision to violate him with full knowledge of

the end result. The real "bad guy" ended up to be the contractor. It was his blueprint for white-collar crime that set the rip-off in motion.

Others were at fault and committed terrible wrongs. But the moral contract was first and foremost violated by the contractor.

The Debriefing Worksheet is helpful in placing and calibrating appropriate doses of blame. After James sued the contractor, he reported:

> The contractor was incredible. At every turn he lied. He contradicted himself in the middle of sentences. He never complied with discovery. There was always an excuse as to why he couldn't supply documents. They had just "computerized." They were "attempting to locate." He was a walking white-collar crime wave.
>
> The documents proved that his license had been removed and he'd been paid a fabricated $250,000 several times over. The story was so good that he used the same scenario, with minor variation, to be paid again and again. It wouldn't take a genius to expose him. "Yet, in court the bastard always got the evidence held out and was coddled. Some technicality blocked the truth and his attorneys called me a thief and a liar in open court," reported James.

Blaming is part of the loved one's post-crime experience as well. Often those who love the victim will self-blame and will have the need to attribute the crime. Sometimes these will be contradictory. Friends and family will feel responsible and protective. Loved ones sometimes blame the victim. The worst remain the old standard responses: the "I told you so's" ; the "Why didn't you's"; and, the "You should have's."

Constructive blame is tricky. Blaming is a moral concept. It is not to be confused with retribution and revenge. A moral law was violated and someone or some entity was responsible. When a series of violations have occurred, isolating the most beneficial target for blame is challenging.

If all of the participants are listed, they can be qualified. The most critical element is to find who made the decision to violate the moral contract with full knowledge that the act would cause suffering. Then, it becomes the duty of the offended to blame according to the values of the victim and the society in which he lives. Until the victim feels better, blame is not finished.

Questions need to be asked as to benefit or harm to national mental health of a blameless society. Where does lying appropriately fit in the overall scheme of blame for committing wrongful acts? What effect does "no fault" have on individuals and institutions? The individual is left with few effective means in civilized society for meeting his fundamental need for justice. After an assault, deep down inside of the victim, a blaming process will begin. The natural course of blaming is to be welcomed by those who care about the LAS victim's recovery and care about society as a decent place in which to live.

Frustrations of Blaming

Victims complain that injustice stings when:

1. A prison sentence is given and later reduced or the offender is able to manipulate his way to early parole.

2. Millions of dollars are spent defending the criminal and the victim ends up broke and cast aside by the system.

3. The victim is not allowed to face the offender with a statement or have a say in his parole or alteration of sentence.

4. The punishment fits the criminal uniquely, not the crime across the board with predictable consistent punishment—country club prisons.

5. The offender gets away with wrongs due to technicalities.

6. Society does not stand up for victims.

7. Delays cause "cruel and unusual punishment" for the victim while favoring the criminal.

8. The moral issues of right and wrong are not addressed.

9. Behavior is not corrected in the future.

10. The victim never gets to tell the "truth and the whole truth" in some manner.

11. The victim never can feel that his post-assault actions have helped to immunize society against the specific type of wrong that he's suffered from.

12. Cost of court transcripts are prohibitive, preventing the exercise of right to an appeal (James' required $8,000 if he was to appeal).

13. Sanctions of huge dollar amounts are put on the *pro se* litigant, preventing them from using the court.

14. Juries are manipulated by judges or their verdicts are ignored or distorted.

15. Attorneys boycott them because they do not have adequate money to meet attorneys' demands.

Chapter 7

Deshaming
Shame Shifted from the Innocent to the Guilty

Lying feeds power. Kant says of lying:
"By a lie a man throws away and, as it were, annihilates his dignity as a man"
(Immanuel Kant, Doctrine of Virtue - Bok)

Deshaming means exactly what it implies, getting rid of shame. Victims inappropriately feel guilty, incompetent, and blameworthy. They suffer sensations of disgrace, dishonor, and regret. Shame reflects distortions of emotions that are common in the lives of victims who fall on the conscience end of the scale (illustrated below). Let's look at human motivation and interaction in the light of wrongful shaming and healthy deshaming.

CONTINUUM of CONSCIENCE vs. POWER
Motivation of Human Behavior

◄── CONSCIENCE CENTERED ———————————— POWER CENTERED ──►

Life's transactions are intersections of behaviors motivated by varying combinations of conscience and power. Mother Teresa is an example of a person of extreme conscience-centered (CC) motivation and Saddam Hussein exemplifies the farthest end of the power-centered (PC) scale. Most people will find their motivations clumping somewhere around the middle. Conscience has nothing to do

---

CC = Motivated by conscience, PC = Motivated by power.

with "bleeding heart," meek or mild personalities. CC's are often aggressive, competitive, powerful individuals. However, they operate within a set of guidelines. Conscience-centered people can have power and can desire power in order to achieve their objectives. However, they differ from the power-centered whose only objective *is* power.

Remember, inappropriate shame results from feeling defenseless in the face of power. If you are wronged and then find yourself suffering shame and guilt, we can be confident that a hostage condition exists which was created by power differential. Control has been lost over some part of life.

Trust has usually left the CC vulnerable. If deception is to work, there have to be those who trust. Convergence of power-centered and conscience-centered people, in their purest forms, will inevitably result in the conscience-centered person being victimized. It is a marriage of deathly complementary value systems upon which the power-centered thrive. They literally tend a garden of trusting relationships while perpetrating hidden agendas.

Those who value truth, honesty, and a moral and ethical code make up the majority of people. These masses are the conscience-centered who collide head-on against a slick minority of individuals, the power-centered. PC's pull out the "big guns" of moral turpitude for power motives, regardless of damage to others or society. I am struck by the vast and silent destruction that results from the invisible clash between the person motivated by power, and the conscience-based individual.

Victims are often the most surprised at both the physical and non-physical injuries with which they are now plagued. If they report their symptoms, they are usually misdiagnosed and misunderstood. They are called depressed, self-pitying, fatigued, or stressed. Victims are treated inaccurately because our society has been slow to recognize the connection between invisible crimes and health.

Invisible wounds have never been part of the media's portrayal of crime. Nothing in schools or professional curriculums has educated the individual as to the health risks of seeking justice. Even when we are aware of PTSD, symptoms are not easily recognized as the psycholegal aspects of PTSD victimization. Likewise, members of a community usually minimize the pain of shame or miss it completely. Unexpectedly, LAS victims enter a tunnel of trauma in which the reverberation from the assault is relentless. High expectations of our justice systems only increase the devastation when a victim enters a real courtroom.

Especially in a rigorous capitalistic society, power behaviors yield a higher payoff than conscience behaviors in the short term. Therefore, America is seeing rampant victimization of the largest segment of our population through scams and corruption. Human application of basic concepts of cooperation, competition, morals, opportunity, Constitutional rights, and quality of life are the threatened psychic underpinnings of our time.

These concepts were put to game theory in a tournament at the University of Toronto. A game was developed called *"Prisoner's Dilemma"* (Axelrod). It relates to LAS because the "prisoner" in the game is created from betrayal ("defection" is the word used for betrayal in Prisoner's Dilemma) like the hostage condition of LAS. The player who follows the rules and cooperates or competes within the guidelines is faced with a possible attack or defection that violates all cooperative efforts. The defector becomes a power-motivated player who violates cooperation in order to take a point advantage over the cooperative player.

Prisoner's Dilemma

The players in Prisoner's Dilemma choose to cooperate or defect over no particular issue. Since there is no purpose or cause except to win points, the motivation that is tapped is pure. Each player looks at a card (illustrated below) and then chooses to place his finger on the box that indicates cooperation or defection. The other player simultaneously chooses a column, again either cooperating or defecting. When put together, their choices result in one of the four possible outcomes shown below.

The Prisoner's Dilemma

		Column Player	
		Cooperate	**Defect**
Row Player	**Cooperate**	R = 3, R = 3 Reward for Mutual Cooperation	S = 0, T = 5 Sucker' Payoff and Temptation to Defect
	Defect	T = 5, S = 0 Temptation to Defect and Sucker's Payoff	P = 1, P = 1 Punishment for Mutual Defection

Note: The payoffs to the Row Chooser are listed first.

Figure 6 - The Prisoner's Dilemma Game Card

If both players cooperate, both do fairly well. Both get an R, the reward for "mutual cooperation." The value is 3 points each. If one player cooperates but the other defects, the defecting player gets the "temptation to defect" worth 5 points, while the cooperating player gets the "sucker's payoff" worth 0 points. If both defect, both get 1 point, the "punishment for mutual defection."

The objective of the game was to gather as many points as possible as impulsively motivated as possible. Surprisingly, the winner of the tournament was "tit for tat." The winning strategy started with a cooperative mode being set down and, thereafter, the first player did whatever the opponent did. If each cooperated, a tacit rule of cooperation was established. Based upon this consistent behavior, trust eventually became a factor in the course of the game.

The results suggest that the more cooperative moves were played, the more stable was the trust. Therefore, long-term interaction is assumed to be a major factor in stabilizing cooperation and building trust. On the other hand, "first blood" and "first injured" defections shattered the stability of the game. The first to deceive often found defection reciprocated. The entire relationship then shifted to retaliatory moves. It is obvious that wars of attrition can easily destroy both players.

Such defections also altered the perceptions and behaviors of all who interacted with the players. "First injured" suffered an immediate image change from player to loser in the eyes of the community. Interestingly, the "community" around the players behaved negatively toward the victim as its members witnessed the PC's defections.

Further, there was contagion of punitive behaviors among community members. The victim was now apt to receive injury from many sources. Mayer cited a manufacturer beginning to have financial difficulty being denied payment by his best customers for merchandise. Therefore, if one is not seen as a force to be reckoned with in the future, that influential posture which demands fair dealing might be lost. "Lame duck" status is awarded to all who appear to falter. It becomes an open door to exponential attacks and spurning (Axelrod).

PC deceivers zero in on the CC person's sensitivity, vulnerability, and desire for cooperation. As PC's move in for the "kill," instinctively they seem to know that their vicious assaults are sure to damage the victim's image. Reckless strategy includes rumors, slander, libel, accusations, stealing of assets, forcing bankruptcy, filing harassing motions, lawsuits or charges, damage to one's credit, threats, business interference, spying, blackmail, and other sleazy moves. This kind of tactical subterfuge is ruinous, and yet remains largely unactionable in terms of the victim's ability to effectively assuage his damaged reputation.

Dukakis attempted to take the high road in the 1988 campaign for the Presidency of the United States. Media dirty tricks showed the mug shot of convicted murderer Willie Horton as the story of his murderous week-end furlough was told. Michael Dukakis was sensationally portrayed as "soft-on-crime" and an incapable leader. Further damage was done by video presentations of a filthy Boston Harbor. Dukakis refused to respond in kind or to choose a blaming action. George Bush's campaign manager later admitted the wrongdoing when he expressed deathbed regret for the mean-spirited attacks on Michael Dukakis. When death from cancer was imminent, he wished that he had managed the campaign without chicanery.

It appeared that Bill Clinton's campaign staff learned the lesson in 1992. They kept a 24-hour rapid response team on alert to immediately and publicly counter negative attacks. Tit for tat was applied.

LAS victims cannot afford the high road. They must place the blame, select a blaming action, and prepare to counter assaults to remove the shame from themselves. Victims need to apply the following formula for rapid-response to attacks by PCs:

Prepare + Blame + Respond = Deshame

1. Gear up to defend against strategic acts of hatred and assaults by the perpetrator(s). Know CC's from PC's.
2. Prepare for inadvertent assaults by system failures.
3. Blame accurately and productively.
4. Respond with appropriate and creative blaming actions.

First comes the crime and then the strategic hatred that the perpetrator uses to defend the crime. Instead of internalizing shame from the acts of hatred and the further systems failures, immediate tit for tat blaming actions divert the shame.

Shamemakers

Every person feels thoroughly saturated with information on crime and victimization because it dominates entertainment and news. Yet this information, so glaring in daily life, fails to prepare and educate in a meaningful way. If anything misleads the victim, it is media's portrayal of the dedicated detective working into the night researching a case, the heroic attorney passionately speaking for the victim (and vicariously for us all) in court, or the judge who maintains a paternal balance between compassion and law. Realistically, most crimes are not solved and most perpetrators are not around for the blame or confrontation. Unlike victimization on TV, there is usually no beginning and no clear cut end to LAS.

Codependent symptoms exacerbate the hurt. Victims with childhood trauma suffer intensified shame-based flashbacks and misleading feelings of guilt. These are the codependents who are more likely to absorb the shame for all who commit wrongdoings around them. If a wrongdoing is discussed in the presence of codependent CC's, the CCs' faces will flush, their heart rates will accelerate, and the innocent may look miserably guilty.

Conscience Centered — Power Centered

Active Deshaming

The steps to deshaming, discussed below, require an internal modulation of beliefs and emotional responses. The therapeutic process requires that beliefs are measured against the here and now, pragmatic rationality, and reality. Those beliefs that are not integrated into the uniquely personal core of cherished values are relinquished. Some beliefs will have been changed or thrown into confusion by the experience itself. These changes become pivotal in prompting life growth. As a result of the deshaming process, the CC emerges in a better posture to win against the odds. His ability to enforce the rules of fair dealing in personal and business transactions is substantially strengthened.

The court, the purported protector of all that is dear to an American citizen, should be our deshaming device. Yet, like a parent who betrays the child when the child needs protection, the court is undeniably used, at the expense of the victim, by the power-centered to further their objectives. We have well established that the court too often becomes part of the power picture, further shaming the decent and honorable taxpayer. Since we cannot rely upon the justice systems to deshame, let's take a look at the fundamental facts and processes that are represented on the continuum and then explore some steps to help us toward deshaming ourselves.

Traits of Conscience vs Power

CC Traits	PC Traits
Guided by conscience	Guided by need for superiority
Values truth	Values lies
Responsible for actions	Not responsible - Your fault
Strives to be ethical/moral	Chameleon-like
Relationships from heart	Relates/belongs for advantage
Consistent belief system	Focus is on self
Focus outward on a task	Functions to outfox
Positive sum - cooperator	Zero sum - covets
Buys shame	Immune to shame
Spiritual power	Political power

CC's Are Cooperators

Conscience-centered people are cooperators. Cooperation always makes one vulnerable to betrayal, yet nothing of value can be achieved without cooperation. Without trust, cooperation is impossible. Judy, James, and P.J. cooperated with their deceivers. Being trustworthy people, they assumed that they could trust others. Those on the conscience-centered side of the continuum are prone to projecting a sense of trust onto others because trusting is their customary way. They enter transactions with the assumption that human beings relate or contract with others according to given guidelines. It was reasonable for James and John to assume that contracts, federal regulation, lawyer's advice, state and local licensure, and the justice system act to ensure the enforcement of the guidelines as set by contract and law.

CC's are Competitors

Can a conscience-centered person be a competitor or be successful in a competitive society? Absolutely, they are our best competitors. Cooperation and competition are not opposites. As described by Axelrod in *The Evolution of Cooperation,* "positive-sum" people use cooperation and competition within a set of rules. They see others succeed in competitive endeavors, encouraging and stimulating them to succeed as well. Cooperators compete fairly.

PC's Are Zero-Sum

Power-centered people will cheat in order to win. They will use "whatever it takes" to win, thus destroying the spirit of the endeavor. Power-centered people are "zero-sum," meaning, if I have something, the power-centered person will feel a loss. The PC has conceptualized others' gains as direct defeats for him. Envy is the emotion that causes the PC to assume that if the other is winning, they must be losing. This distortion vindicates acts of deception and other sleazy moves. Obviously, the result is an unjust loss for those who played fairly. Vehemently, however, these liars share, with those they betray, the desire not to be deceived.

The power-centered person's striving for significance is limited and distorted. The further toward the power end of the continuum, the more the individual will lack the ability to cooperate. The power-centered are not interested in other people. When they find a problem which demands cooperation with others, it throws them into tension. Since they can't be trusted, they feel incapable of trusting.

Those who pursue power do so from a posture of imagined superiority. They spend their energies outwitting others and the law. Power seekers envision themselves to be more cunning than they are. However, the ability to deprive others of their property, to have command of life and death, to prove one's own importance at the expense of others, and to deceive others creates the sensation of superiority (Tucker).

Power orientation leans toward extremes in self-serving actions and crime. Since the entire direction power strivers take is bold, visible and influential, they will often be politicians, presidents, dictators, and famous leaders in their fields. This brings into focus myths to be dispelled.

MYTH 1: Criminals are often geniuses. Intelligence does not seem to be a factor in crime. It can appear as intelligence because criminals get away with considerable crime before they're caught and their daring can cause them to look heroic or momentarily brilliant. If they're in power, they cover up their crimes through favors and intimidation.

MYTH 2: All public servants serve the public. The PACs (Political Action Committees), the viciousness of campaigning, and the resistance to positive change by those in power, keep CC's out of public service and/or limits their terms. Those with integrity withdraw from public service in droves every year. They point to chicanery, pressure from lobbyists, and difficulty in dealing with their promises to constituents as reasons for withdrawing from public service (Greider). PC's in CC clothing are naturals to sit in a family portrait in front of a flag, and chameleon their way to power.

These types of PC's call the population "stupid" and manipulate polls, images, and votes. In fact, the population of trustworthy CC's are slow to fathom the wiles of PC's, who can look and sound sincere.

CC and PC Traits Vary in All People
Most people find their motives falling near the middle with a tendency toward power or conscience. It is natural to have the incentive to be selfish. It was our Founding Fathers who described men as certainly not being angels. Thus, we face this fundamental issue as we approach our social, political, and economic relationships.

Statistically, it has been shown that mutual cooperation is the key to long term enrichment of both participants. Power-centered players focus on the short term. Therefore, it is critical to know the initial strategy of the other player. If the opponent steps in with deception on the first move, the cooperator can lose everything.

How Do CC's Protect Themselves?
Develop Sight, Insight, and Foresight
"I just didn't see it coming," victims tell me. "How could I have been so blind?" they ask me. Three tasks combine to develop sight, insight, and foresight, the first protective goal.

Task 1 - See the game. See both players, in your mind's eye, on the continuum. Don't be blinded by dreams, hopes, or wants, but be aware of what you want, specifically. Don't buy verbal promises and don't act too fast. Take time for history to develop through a few moves.

Task 2 - Gain insight into the motives of the other player. Even if the first few moves are cooperative, caution is in order. When you know what you want and what motivates you, then ask yourself, "What motivates the other player?"

Task 3 - Verify every statement and document. Trust if you wish, but verify nevertheless.

Visualizing human beings in transactions on the continuum helps discern just where on the scale the other player falls in terms of his motivation.

Don't Envy or Emulate

Envy is the weakness of the power-centered person. Regardless of what this person achieves in life, he will always feel envious. He is devoid of joy. If you have anything, he will be distressed because he doesn't have it. Power people spend their time comparing themselves to others and coveting what the other has. They feel so miserable that it becomes a justification to reach out and take. Envy is a self-destructive emotion.

Reciprocate Cooperation

Tit for tat won the tournament mentioned above. Yet tit for tat never once scored better in a game than the other player. It can't, since it only responds to the defection of the other player. Therefore, tit for tat will achieve the same score or less than the other player. It is a non zero-sum activity. Never did one player have to do better than the other in order to do well for himself. Doing well for oneself and focusing on that goal proved far more successful than striving to do better than the other player.

Retaliate Power Moves With Blaming Actions, Immediately

A common theme that runs through counseling sessions with LAS victims is how much they've endured before they really got angry or took negative action. Reluctance to give way to anger is seen as a virtue with many of these patients. Yet the behaviors displayed in the game theory that we're exploring suggest that immediate response to provocation is most effective at turning the game back to cooperative moves.

It might also appear from the game theory that cooperative moves are always the best, even better than tit for tat. Unconditional cooperation seems to CC's to be more right than tit for tat. The problem with taking the lofty road of "turning the other cheek" is that it provides incentive for the other player to exploit you. The power-centered get "drunk with power" when such opportunities present themselves time and time again. Such adherence to cooperation creates monsters. PC's can't resist the urge to ambush the vulnerable. Everyone becomes prey.

Each player must make it hard to be exploited. Insisting upon fair play is a fundamental element of reciprocity. Therefore, by a simple tit for tat game plan, cooperation is always positively rewarded and deception is immediately attacked with a blaming action. The CC's standard of a competent blaming action is one which reinforces the moral code. It sounds a little like an "eye for an eye," but it does not degrade the blamer. Rather, the reciprocating CC chooses a method that brings the defector more into alignment with the good that is unquestionably sanctioned by society. Such actions serve society and also prevent an echoing feud.

Streamline Your Shame Base

> Clear your mind. Then forget foundationless traditions, forget the "moral" standards others may have tried to cram down your throat, forget the beliefs people may have tried to intimidate you into accepting as "right." Allow your intellect to take control as you read, and, most important, think of yourself - Number One - as a unique individual.
> (Ringer, *Looking Out for Number One*)

Robert Ringer leads you into his book with this quote. It is designed to shake the foundations that keep the CC from coping with the PC in the world of business. While it is fresh and direct, the CC simply can't divorce himself from moral boundaries to the extent that he functions as another PC. However, every LAS victim that I've worked with has had some degree of shame-based burden that he was able to peel off. This is the target of streamlining the shame-base.*

---

*The foundation of shame is supported by a person's belief system.

James held a meeting to analyze the failings of the contractor prior to requesting the bank's cooperation in firing the contractor. At the conclusion of the meeting, James summarized his decision to confront the contractor, presented a list of tasks to be done, and basically gave him one more chance. He shares that his reasoning had to do with the contractor being a family man, with children, who was having problems. Perhaps the human route would buy loyalty, improved performance and greater understanding between them.

James shed two outdated concepts of his belief system during deshaming. First, men who support families and the problems of the men's families no longer have a place in James' belief system. He realized that his father had taught him this principle in childhood. There was an assumption that men with families would be similarly motivated to be decent and needed a break. James now could see that this bumbling contractor with the angelic stance was a purebred PC. Secondly, giving PC's breaks allow PC's time to get a further foothold into such a project. The time delay caused by this decision was critical to James' economic demise.

It is important to examine the concepts that have been embraced by the LAS victim. When we are taught our values in childhood we conceptualize from the data presented by the big world around us. An example (Financial Management):

When we think of flying, we think of birds. Man

envied the bird...and all efforts to create flight were based on bird observations. The airplane today is a copy of the bird, except for the power plant.

Is it true that in order to be aerodynamically sound an object must have wings? No. A rocket and bullets fly on power alone. If you put a hundred aerosol insecticide bombs in your house and set them all off, your house will fly too. The initial data was good information. However, the conceptualization was limiting for those who adhered to the wing theory. Time changes, economics change; we've moved from a stable to a transient society, and new data abounds daily. Open-mindedness means flexibility in re-examining concepts as we greet the future.

Old beliefs or concepts put to new realities act as masochism, when failure and victimization compound. Society misunderstands when mistakes are repeated. Victims appear to "need" their victimization or to "ask for it" by adhering to the Commandments, the "Golden Rule," or "respectable behaviors" as taught by their parents.

The Story of Manny

An older gentleman named Manny asked to speak to me one day. He knew of the work I was doing with victims and he shared a horror story of intimidation and white collar crime. He was stuck in a belief system that had been taught to him by his father's actions and words. His father was an independent cab driver in New York who'd been approached by gangsters who threatened him. He stood up to them with spirit and courage and won their respect. They protected his turf and he did well as an independent cab driver throughout the raising of his children.

He taught them to "stand up for their rights.'"Manny's assets had been taken from him by judgments obtained by a white-collar criminal. He was sure that the judge and the criminal were in cahoots. He tried to use his father's teachings to stand up to the judge. He told the judge what he believed his rights were and then, when he began to feel totally helpless, threatened the judge.

The FBI called on him and began to follow him. He said he got a gun to protect himself. He was frightened at being overpowered. His bank accounts had been taken, his properties were taken, his ability to earn a living had ceased, and he was without resources.

He attended one group and then disappeared. During the group interaction, it was obvious that he was attempting to live up to his fathers' expectations of a "real man." A modern milieu does not reward standing up to the powerful in a direct manner. He had trouble hearing that feedback from the group. We are left wondering whatever happened to Manny.

Manny needed to streamline dangerous confrontations from his belief system. Courage needed re-alignment in Manny's world.

Deshaming redefines courage. Is it more courageous to take a loss and stick with your beliefs, or to be flexible and bend with rationality? It is not as difficult as it sounds to sort out the core values that one would break a relationship over or die for versus those that were good at a different place, in a different time with the knowledge that was available at that time.

This is a good time to go back to the debriefing sheet and look at the victim's list. Ask again, "What did I believe before victimization and what do I believe now?" Some beliefs will cause sadness when they are let go. Beliefs about justice and our leaders and patriotic values are losses to victims as they face the rationality of today. It is masochistic, however, to enter a courtroom or make a critical decision without the candid and brutal facts, regardless of how bitter those facts may taste.

Stick with your Conscience

Sometimes it seems like the bad guys get all the goodies and the good guys always come up short. Financial Management Associates put out a book in 1976 called Why S.O.B.s Succeed and Nice Guys Fail in a Small Business. It is a classic on PC tactics and advises the CC to adopt more of the PC's attitudes and behaviors. It can become tempting to use the wiles of the power-motivated in order to even the score. Further, by the time the criminals have had their way with the victims, the victims have become exquisitely knowledgeable about deceptive maneuvers. James knows the anatomy and physiology of white-collar crime thoroughly. He also has earned a "street Ph.D." in abuses of the court system for personal gain.

Character and integrity are the issues at this juncture. As patients swore that they were going to loosen their ethical standards, and then didn't, I've wondered what glue kept them stuck to their consciences. It truly is born out that values from early childhood dictate our behavior for a lifetime. It is probably hopeful, because those with honorable intentions in life are hard to corrupt. Patients have demonstrated to me that humans cherish the moral matrix of their beings, once the masochistic, superfluous societal expectations are removed. Their behaviors, regardless of consequences, then bring joy and inspiration.

PC's, who are driven by envy and fear, never know esteem. Especially if they are at the far end of the scale, and regardless of blaming actions or society's efforts, the power motivated may never buy into the moral code. Others whose motives are more moderate can be profoundly effected by thorough blaming actions. However, the more they are PC-motivated, the less they are touched by emotional, moral or ethical issues.

Correctional systems, it seems, are only partially effective with PC's, and then only if: (1) they're caught, (2) they're indicted, (3) they're convicted, and (4) the crime is punished consistently, giving the criminal no individual consideration. PC's are willing to change if they can depend upon being inconvenienced every time they commit the offense, in spite of circumstances. If this inconvenience happens each time they become deceptive players, we can more confidently gamble that a simple uplifting conditioning is possible. Extreme PC's can never be expected to give up their crime-styles or uncooperative behaviors due to an awakening of a moral code. They will refrain simply because it is no longer beneficial, convenient or self-serving to continue deceptive behavior.

Focus on the Simple Facts of Wrongdoing

The thrust of court proceedings and the trail of cover-up become a quagmire of technical jargon and remote issues totally unrelated to the facts of the crime or the truth. No one wants to hear reality as the victim knows it, except the victim. Even his attorney enters the twisted trail of legal jargon, because it is what he knows best and it causes control to be removed from the litigant. If he can work the truth into it, the victim is fortunate.

> Part of this problem is dealing with people in terms of what they consider rational. Rationality is the ability to perceive things as they really are. In a gambling casino the odds are rigged heavily in favor of the house. Anybody gambling in that casino is essentially irrational in terms of reality. However, the man or woman there who is cheating, in order to bring the odds in their favor, is acting rationally. It is considered both immoral and illegal but it is rational (Financial Management).

When lawyers behave in a manner that is only rational to them, CC's become incensed. Sometimes, overwhelmed by outrage, they become immobile. Nothing prepares them for the fact that their attorney will enter a never-never land of selfishly rational behavior in the courtroom. All court personnel coolly execute legalese upon the victim. Victims are left without skills and without representation in terms of reality as they perceive it. The chameleon PC is a natural for court. Here it has become rational for the guilty party to lie and gnarl the facts.

This type of contest can teach us another lesson from tit for tat. The high road in court does not buy the respect and favor of the judge. Turning the other cheek will usually buy nothing but two bruised cheeks instead of one.

> After years of delays, James was eager to get to court. He was right; he had the evidence; and, you know the story. His presentation was ready. After the evidence was held out and he'd been called, in open court by opposing counsel, every dreaded name he could imagine, the contractor was found to not be guilty or liable for the damages.
>
> At this juncture, the trustee's attorney took the results of the contractor's trial and lied in a letter to the U.S. Attorney. The trustee's attorney applied the judge's decision regarding the contractor to the suit against the bank. They were two separate cases. It was a clear deception, but the U.S. Attorney bought it and did no further investigation of the trustee's and bank's fraudulent actions.

James was uncomfortable at being forced to endure abuse and play the court game. Attorneys call it "managing their clients" or "keeping their clients under control." This means that whatever attorneys choose to do with the case or the truth, the client will cooperate and happily pay for the results. If ever there was a power-differential set up to abuse an individual and assault his mental health, it is found in the pictures of James and John caught in the squeeze between their attorneys, the opposition's attorneys, greedy takers, and a judge who does not protect their civil rights.

Set Up Your Own System of Determining Credibility and Components of Establishing Trustworthiness.

PC's who are experienced at conning the system have credit reports, financial statements, references, and licensing under their control. The chapter on empowerment will deal with the specific skills that have helped other victims gain the most important data that cannot be easily manipulated by PC's.

> James determined the PC contractor's credibility based upon a state license as a building contractor, a financial statement, tax returns, a Dunn and Bradstreet rating of the company, a credit report, and the fact that, when he inquired as to any complaints at the State Contractor's Board office, the computer showed that there had never been a complaint.
>
> After he was in litigation, James subpoenaed the contractor's file to find a 13 year history of crime with exactly the same M.O. as in James' victimization. The file was full of complaints, hearings, suits, and pleas to the Contractor's Board to do its job. Millions of dollars had been stolen over more than a decade.

We're in a time when the usual methods of attaining knowledge about a person's character are dangerously inaccurate.

CC's and PC's rationality and reality are diametrically opposed. LAS victims cannot and choose not to change their values. It is hard for them to comprehend valuing material goods over the very moral core of the CC's being. However, since most of us will fall toward the middle, with power and conscience in a dynamic balancing act, we can examine, re-align, and become more operative in our own best interest. Modulation, a term used in music, means a transition of key, going from one key to another, by a certain succession of chords, either in a natural and flowing manner, or sometimes in a sudden and unexpected manner. It accommodates the tone to a certain degree of intensity, light, or shade. The deshaming process causes a modulation of beliefs wherein the victim remains essentially the same, in terms of values, but modulations of beliefs and values bring life-growth with self acceptance, elasticity, wisdom, and effective use of spiritual power.

Chapter 8

Reframing
A Pivotal Process

"A man is measured by the expanse of the moral horizon he chooses to inhabit."
Sandor McNab (Fire in the Belly)

The five processes, debriefing, grieving, obsession, deshaming and blaming, bring us to the point of reframing. Each step has prepared us for this chapter. Reframing is the pivotal procedure whereby we embark on the final phase toward recovery.

Reframing cannot be done immediately following the trauma. Until the first five processes are completed, attempts at reframing will not be optimal. The idea is to take the individual's perceptions that lend to damaged self esteem, to a sense of vulnerability, or to shame, and reframe the picture with insights that empower, reduce anxiety, and affirm self.

The victim shifts from a painful perception of self, as a result of the incident, to a new, open, morally sound, and personally inspired view. When this is done in a group, I have the group applaud the statement of the reframed insight (examples below). It is helpful to reframe in a group or with a therapist because the affirming reactions of others validate our reframed image of self. It feels like a new self; in fact, it is a perceptually rearranged self. Victims need to believe the reframed selves. Therefore, the reframing must be based on real strengths of the individual and accurate observations.

It has not been difficult to find rich personal assets among the victims. Facts point to there being something very right about victims. Bard and Sangrey state, "The good person is the logical target of the predator. The lion hunts the gazelle, the lovely one." Those of culture, artistic talent, scientific excellence, and academic scholarship often do not perceive the threat of the power-centered individual. Hard working, kind, and generous citizens aren't greeting their world with suspicion.

The conscience-centered person cannot and does not seek power through acts or beliefs that betray his deep-rooted values. Empowerment of the talented, thoughtful, and learned must be accomplished within the boundaries of their value systems. The challenge is to empower from a conscience-centered stance. It can be done. Mother Teresa, for example, has great power and has functioned beautifully within her value system and against tough odds.

Gaining power through special interest groups, political favors, lies, and greed are distasteful and immoral to many who've been victimized. They simply can't adopt actions that contradict their values. Some may stray for a time, but the reframe endures that aligns with the victim's moral conscience. In my counseling practice I have often noted the effectiveness of reframing in reconfirming victims' fine qualities while discouraging the creation of a new self.

LAS Reframe Checklist

Rate the intensity and frequency of the following emotional reactions/responses to the traumatic incidents in your experience. Use 1 for sometimes, 2 for most of the time and 3 for profoundly felt and interfering with normal activity.

Legal Abuse Syndrome

1. _____ trapped
2. _____ creativity hampered
3. _____ wiped out
4. _____ anxious about future
5. _____ stressed out
6. _____ troubled
7. _____ crushed
8. _____ guilty
9. _____ mistrust people
10. _____ worthless
11. _____ withdrawn
12. _____ punished
13. _____ unhappy
14. _____ weary
15. _____ stupid
16. _____ at loose ends
17. _____ life is irrational
18. _____ the system doesn't work
19. _____ outraged
20. _____ why?
21. _____ why me?
22. _____ inadequate
23. _____ resentful
24. _____ rejected
25. _____ abandoned
26. _____ angry
27. _____ depressed
28. _____ numb
29. _____ isolated

30. _____ exhausted
31. _____ unenthusiastic
32. _____ defensive
33. _____ embarrassed
34. _____ afraid
35. _____ resigned
36. _____ disappointed
37. _____ cyclical, in a rut
38. _____ abusing alcohol or drugs
39. _____ compulsive/overeating etc.
40. _____ leaning on prescription drugs
41. _____ workaholic/keeps busy
42. _____ TV/couch are companions
43. _____ insomnia/worried about sleeping
44. _____ physical symptoms
45. _____ daydreaming/mentally escaping
46. _____ intellectualizing/rigid/formal/clinical
47. _____ avoids closeness with people/intimacy

Add any others that bother you and then reframe them according to the following exercise.

Reframing Exercise

First, look at the feeling or symptom. Put it in a self-appraising statement, i.e., if "physical symptoms" was checked with a 3. the self-appraising statement might be, "I'm too sick to be desirable to another person." Or if you checked "defensive," "I must have done something wrong to deserve this." Take these sentences through the three-step process:

1. List perceptions to be reframed.

2. Write out the reframed perception.

3. Acknowledge wisdom gained from the experience. "As a result of this experience, I will never....again." "Because this happened, I'm becoming a person who...." (Flanigan)

Example 1.

1. Initial perception.

    "I was a fool."

2. Reframed.

    "I'm a trustworthy person. I believed that others were largely trustworthy too."

3. Wisdom gained.

    "Because this happened, I'm becoming a person who checks out everything in a business deal. I leave nothing to the other person's word. I feel sad that I can't trust others but I choose not to take unnecessary risks."

Example 2.

1. Initial perception.

    "I'm so ashamed. How can I face my (wife) (family) (colleagues)?"

2. Reframed.

"I refuse to bear the shame that belongs on the criminal or the person who abused power and violated the moral code."

3. Wisdom gained.

"As a result of this experience, I'm becoming aware that I tend to suffer from inappropriate shame. Because this happened, I will blame the wrong-doer more and myself less in the future."

Example 3.

1. Initial perception.

"I should have seen it coming. How could I have been so stupid?"

2. Reframed.

"I was not responsible to be paranoid or omniscient. I'm an intelligent person who did not suspect wrongdoing."

3. Wisdom gained.

"Intelligence, contracts, or the law do not protect us from con artists. In the future, I'll run when I suspect power moves."

Example 4.

1. Initial perception.

    "I couldn't take it if I ever got betrayed again. I couldn't stand it."

2. Reframed.

    "All decent people are vulnerable to betrayal. It would hurt to be deceived again, but to not take judicious risks is to be dead."

3. Wisdom gained.

    "In the future, I'm going to depend less on others for my feeling of being complete."

Example 5.

1. Initial perception.

    "I should have protected my property better and it would not have been stolen. I guess I asked for it."

2. Reframed.

    "The criminal was dead wrong for coming into my space and stealing my property. I will prosecute to the fullest extent of the law."

3. Wisdom gained.

   "As a result of this experience, I will install more locks and an alarm system."

Example 6.

1. Initial perception.

   "The criminal was sure smarter than I was. He knew how to manipulate the system."

2. Reframed.

   "I spend my time and energy contributing to society. It is hard to anticipate the actions of someone who spends his time and energy intending to abuse and do harm. The system was used inappropriately."

3. Wisdom gained.

   "I cannot depend on the system to protect me. I must use every avenue that a citizen can muster to force reform."

Example 7.

1. Initial perception.

   "Being good bought me nothing. There is no justice."

2. Reframed.

    "I'm a person with fine values who strives for excellence. I still value living a just life in this unjust world and will do so in my personal life."

3. Wisdom gained.

    "Goodness, decency and excellence don't buy clout. When I must have clout, I'll not expect my fine reputation to buy it. The power-centered attorney I may need to hire for court clout does not have to suit my standard of decency or have my personal respect... a tough decision."

Example 8.

1. Initial perception.

    "I'm fighting a huge bank. What chance do I have against their power?"

2. Reframed.

    "Corporations abuse power by their very structure and focus on a bottom line. I'm a moral person, who doesn't choose to use trickery or underhanded tactics in my dealings. I'm at a distinct disadvantage against these people in the courts."

3. Wisdom gained.

"There is a foundation that supports the corporate bottom line. That foundation is composed of consumers. I will become a Vigilante Consumer, as described by Faith Popcorn." (See Vigilante Consumerism in Chapter on Empowerment)

Goals of Successful Reframing
<u>From Victim to Veteran</u>

No longer will the LAS victim define himself by the traumatic experience. He will reframe the self-image from "I was the victim of..." to "I am a veteran and a successful survivor of a clear wrongdoing." The flaws of the offended will no longer be the main focus after reframing. Likewise, the horror story will not be the topic (or the avoided topic) in conversation. A newly emerged self will be presented with ease. Perspective replaces the obsessive struggle of the hostage.

Tom and his family planned to move from Florida to Connecticut. They negotiated to buy a house, prepared to move, and discovered that their new house did not have clear title. Liens had been filed on it and the transaction was in jeopardy. They retained an attorney who assured them that they could go forward. The owners of the property had declared bankruptcy and the court guaranteed that it would provide clear title.

After a period of time, pressure was on the family to move. Their attorney prepared an interim lease/purchase agreement. The vans were loaded, the move was accomplished, and the keys were turned over to Tom. They moved in believing that the house was tacitly theirs. They made the improvements required in order to make the house habitable. Water supply systems needed repair and other equally vital maintenance was required.

The Connecticut attorney for the seller was in monthly communication, providing a paper trail that assured Tom clear title would be presented at closing time. The attorney also advised the family to hold lease payments until the liens were removed. This all had a credible tone to it. Several months passed. Tom's family decided to contact the seller directly to spur on the purchase. Stunned, Tom was told that the seller knew nothing of the lease/purchase and thought the home was vacant. Tom advised the seller to talk to the seller's Connecticut attorney who had represented him in the transaction. In two days, an odyssey would begin that would forever change Tom's family's life.

We will follow Tom from the depths of victimization to an effectively reframed self. Each reframe goal was achieved by Tom.

From Disillusioned Belief System To Suffusion of Firm Moral Foundation

"Okay, I accept; I own this horror." "I had no control; my belief in the trustworthiness of most people was my undoing." "I can't be a power-centered individual; I am still vulnerable and I'm scared." "I don't like the facts of life that victimization has taught me." "I truly felt happier before I knew, even though I'm wiser now."

These are statements made by victims as they faced the need to surrender to the truth around us and to recognize the limits of our abilities to control life's incidents. Each one demonstrates natural resistance to painful facts. Once the victim accepts the ugly, hostage/perpetrator fact of life, it can be reframed to bring the power of the moral code back to empower the side of the victim.

When the victim is first taken emotional hostage, he becomes morally lost. During the invisible assault, no one is tending to the moral code. There is a period of time when the moral and ethical facets of human behavior break down completely.

Morality and ethics continue to be neglected in the aftermath. Legalized right and wrong replace moral and ethical standards, especially during litigation. Systems rarely respond to the moral or ethical issues involved in wrongdoing. James reported the appropriate crimes to the FBI. When James and his wife mentioned ethical violations, the top man in the white-collar crime unit snarled and sighed. The lawyers in James' case never addressed moral or ethical matters in the 10 years of his legal struggles. The attorney for the trustee told James that the court had "nothing to do with justice or right or wrong, only what was actionable."

Yet, as we work through each step on our path out of rage, we find that the moral code forms the basis for most regulations, rules, contracts, and many laws. When we begin to manage our lives again, the moral foundation can be reframed to suit our new perspective. As we move toward empowerment, our moral code ideally will be projected outward. We are no longer winner versus loser, but, reframed, we are now an abuser of power vs. a moral and decent, conscience-centered individual.

From Disconnected to Networking with Others of Conscience

Look deeply inside and you will find that victims shun love and support from others. Surrounding every victim are loved ones whose warm efforts have been coldly rejected. The victim closes down emotionally. The veteran begins to open up and risks feeling again. Relationships will repair if they have a thread of connectedness left. Sometimes it is too late and the relationship has been broken by the LAS syndrome.

A sad but comforting certainty lies in the multitude of victims generated in our society. James has a ready resource of emotional comfort, validation, and information that is helpful. He networks with an ever-growing number of victims of bankruptcy fraud across America. They are invariably conscience-centered people with fine intelligence, usually well educated, entrepreneurial, and always ambitious.

Most of the group members are victims of bankruptcy court abuses. The network is loosely organized in terms of supporting one another's efforts with letters, phone calls, and faxes. They exchange legal information, professional referrals, and ideas for recovery. Networking also saves time. James believes that at the rate citizens are being victimized, it will be the largest representation in history if they ever organize and point their efforts toward political or social change.

Grass roots organizations abound. Many are interlocking memberships in order to gain potency through numbers. Membership costs are usually small and the networking potential is rich. Some organizations are listed. (See Appendix B)

<u>From a Sense of Loss to Free and Ready to Fill the Void</u>
We did not choose to lose our beliefs or belongings. Now that they are gone, the opportunity exists to fill the void. We are purged and absolved of old responsibilities, naiveté, and our past lifestyle. There is an Oriental expression that in every loss there is a gain and in every gain, a loss. The gain is emphasized during this reframing exercise.

From your losses, list the gains. This does not mean "a look on the bright side;" it is the maximizing of your strengths required for recovery. Neither does it minimize the wrong that was done or the magnitude of losses. Extracting gain from loss is a vital habit that survivors use to force benefit from suffering. It greatly enhances recovery.

James sat in his expansive recreation room on a bar stool at his wetbar and shared with his wife that the court had converted him to Chapter 7 liquidation. All of their assets were at risk, regardless of his strong evidence and objections. That was almost a decade ago. Now, as he looks back, he remembers his wife asking, "Do you think you might lose me and your family too - along with everything else?" He had responded that it was a fear. Now he sees that the family did not abandon him when their comfortable lifestyle was lost. In fact, they have all worked extremely hard together to fight the battle and to survive. James went from running three corporations to housecleaner, chef, and chauffeur of the children. All the while he has fought in court and tried to rebuild his business. His wife has worked three jobs at times in order to support the family. Certainly, his gain came in an unwelcome package. However, the testing of this family provides a gain in trust and confidence that empowers his endeavors during his recovery.

Tom appreciates gains from external sources. Tom lost his attorney and found himself without funds to hire another. He felt desperate, filled with principle and indignation, but was without a gatekeeper to the court. Tom began to study the law and prepare his own legal documents. He has represented himself in court based upon the foundations of the judicial system. As Thoreau learned and became centered from Walden Pond in a milieu of chosen isolation, Tom's innermost self unfolded in forced isolation. His predicament, history text, computer, and lawbooks were his mentors. He has emerged equally centered. Thoreau emerged from Walden Pond rich in his knowedge of his world and his place in it. Tom's gains are several-pronged. He is centered as to the truth and his commitment to his principles. He is deeply in love with his Country and the design of its government. This veteran of wrongdoing is patient and clear about his mission. He will die, go to jail, and work long hours in poverty, if necessary, in order to correct an aberration that threatens his precious form of government. His fine research and sound legal work are readily shared with others. Tom appreciates the victimized citizens as gifts, further gaining from his losses.

Reframing directly confronts the loss of confidence and the paralysis of dreams. It takes the sweeping, immobilizing perceptions that follow profound victimization and carefully pinpoints the vulnerability that made him (the victim) a target. Reframing then leads to a wisdom that begins the healing; a sort of psychological scar tissue is formed that allows the resuscitation of wants and dreams.

Victims who've been profoundly assaulted by systems they trusted lose consciousness of what they want in life. If asked, they will want just to be left alone, or never to go through such a trauma again. Those are not wants. Wants have to do with life being tasteful, satisfying, and full. Wants allude to the future with vitality. Vulnerability, such as trust, and sweeping assumptions like "I was stupid," cripple and confuse a person's ability to want. Pinpointed reframing statements, i.e., "I was trusting, not stupid," bring a wiser perspective. Reframed perspective allows judicious risk-taking rather than cellophane-wrapped removal from life, and opens the door to wants again.

Begin to generate a list of wants and dreams. As an assignment, victims find this list a most difficult task. Wants and dreams were part of a past perception of life. They depended on a reality that evaporated along with friends, confidence in protective agencies, and systems that proved to be mythical. This list brings with it fear and apprehension. Belief systems that supported past dreams have been shattered. It will feel as if there are barriers to wanting. Nevertheless, this list provides the matrix and energy for the fight that must go on, the meaning of your existence, and the riches yet to come.

From Aging to Down-Aging

There is no good age to be victimized. Any age of adult victimization is too old or too young to have been treated poorly. The good news is that today we can throw out tradition as it relates to age. Futurists tell us that our concepts of age are inaccurate.

Legal Abuse Syndrome

> John is 71 years old. He is also broke and has lost hope of retirement on the assets of his company. He lives on a meager income that is barely subsistent. He talks of going back to masonry or at least hauling to the sites. When he thinks of going back to work at 71, his wife fears for his health and he wonders if he is hirable. We talked to John of down-aging.

Baby boomers started a cultural transformation when they turned 40 around 1986. AARP claims that they represent one-fifth of American voters. Concepts of age have exploded. There is a refusal to be bound by traditional age limitations. The entire concept is supported by increased life expectancy and expenditures on plastic surgery, hair color, anti-wrinkle devices, and fitness equipment. Forty-two percent of the runners in the New York Marathon were over 40. The oldest came in at 91 (Popcorn). Victims feel that they are too old to restart, but facts contradict this.

Actually, we've down-aged about 10 years in terms of health and longevity. Victims need to look at their predicaments using a decade reduction in their ages. In other words, if you are 40 now, you are really more like 30 in terms of how that age behaves, looks, and feels. Therefore, 50 is really 40 and 60 is really 50. The number stays the same, but the behavior and degree of aging process is down-aged 10 years (Popcorn).

Those things we've dreamed of doing are probably still possible. Traditional perceptions of age confine our choices. Major lifestyle changes happen when veterans of wrongdoing open up to down-aging. It is not too late to move, change careers, or develop talents. Try that small business or move to the village beside the lake. Give up the rat race if "getting out" has always been a dream. Take up a new sport or craft. Paint beautiful paintings for a living or live on the boat that you fantasize about. There is still time. John is energetic and very sharp mentally. He is determined to fight his battle and to survive. When I talk to John, he seems much more like 61, or less than 71. There is a gleam in his eye when he speaks of working, especially hauling materials.

From Numb to Receptive to New Ideas, and to Relationships

"Come out and Play" is the theme of Alfred Adask's[5] victims group. All are victims of court and litigation trauma. Alfred encourages victims to come to the groups and to be with others even though their opioids are still numbing in full swing. Numbness does not just dissipate. It eases up in micro-fragments. Participants may only be able to discuss one part of the trauma, but still be in denial or unable to feel the impact of other elements of the injury. It is okay. Start where you can in spite of the obstacles.

A significant barrier to reframing is fear of "bursting the emotional dam." Nature is sensitive in providing our own chemical protection. Without opioids and welcomed desensitization, pain would render us nonfunctional. Unfortunately, the price of numb automated functionality is dullness. Victims deserve better. Let's take the next step now. Let's come out of dullness and gently begin to interact.

One victim judiciously showed up at various groups of mine for 14 years. This lady, after all those years, began reading short emotional paragraphs to the group. The risk was eased by careful preparation of her paragraph during the week. Verbal interaction with the group followed. She began to put her feelings into poems

---

[5] Alfred Adask publishes a magazine titled the "Antishyster." He is one of the ordinary citizens who is not published by a large company or established except by genuine, personal contributions to LAS victims (See appendix B).

and share them with the group.

At last, her "emotional dam" burst. She had feared "letting go" for 14 years. Her catharsis consisted of crying profusely and eating chocolate for the next two sessions while she shared a lifetime of guilt manipulation by her mother. This lady had never been her own person, just her mother's caregiver. She had never developed her talents because her mother was talented in the arts also and she felt too guilty to compete on her mother's artistic turf. Two years later, this woman is aggressively studying art and preparing for her first art show. Fear of crying and the pain of guilt would have prevented her dream of a retirement career as an artist. "Emotional dams" are far more frightening in perception than reality. In twenty years, I've witnessed crying, eating, punching a wall, and pacing. All unlocked wonderful human potential. Take a chance.

Another barrier to reframing is in the resistance to relinquishing numbness. Once the opioids relax, an identity crisis follows. We are not who we were before the assaults. We are not the loser, liar, thief, crybaby, nor disgruntled litigant that our adversaries have characterized. So, who are we? Certainly, after introspection and study, Tom was a centered person who had developed a sound system of reframing.

> Tom had been ridiculed, sanctioned, insulted, and enjoined in his experiences with the court, even though he had won a jury judgement. Finally, his mental health was questioned by the court. Friends treated him impatiently and advised him to give up and get on with life. He was advised by all that this was a "David and Goliath" battle he could

not win. Only a few family members who knew him well encouraged him. They knew that when his principles were assaulted, he had to fight.

As a master of reframing, Tom's statements are roughly as follows: "As a result of these experiences, I'm becoming a person who values my system of government too much to let it be abused by racketeers and to not fight for what is mine. I fought on the beaches of foreign countries to protect my freedom; I'd better be as committed to the cause of freedom when it is jeopardized on my own soil as I was as a soldier. I will not be shamed by the abuse of criminals."

Tom has become a lay expert on the law, the Constitution, and U.S. history. Reframing is a daily occurrence as he must emotionally react to the responses from those in power who degrade his attempts to preserve and enforce his rights. Tom is a fine example of a veteran of wrongdoing. He has been called obsessed and he agrees. Psychologically, Tom works through his pain, and remains realistic, patient, and focused. A few judges along the way have admired his work and been supportive, as have certain law enforcement agents.

From Lack of Validation by Others to Validation of Self

One of the most painful experiences Tom and other LAS victims must overcome is dismissal from the court. Hope is regularly dismissed in the form of calling their lives, their pain, their losses and their interpretation of their protection under the law "FRIVOLOUS" and sometimes "FRIVOLOUS AND WITHOUT MERIT."

Unwanted cases are often deemed "frivolous" by the judges. What is of no meaning to one person may have profound meaning to another. Tom has repeatedly had his painstaking work, the devastation of his life and his hope and trust in his Constitution called "...of little value or importance; trifling; trivial; paltry; not properly serious or sensible; silly and light-minded; or giddy." That is the definition of "frivolous." If any collision in life could explode into rage, it is years of careful and arduous effort risked on your court, your protector, and then to be immediately dismissed as "frivolous." We will follow Tom's response to such dismissals in the next chapter. How does one sustain positive and responsible effort in the face of such outrage?

Without a reframing skill at hand, when the outrage insults us, some will act irrationally. Each assault requires reframing or it accumulates. These are the times when people will arm themselves and walk into an office or agency shooting or drive through the front of a building.

Tom must continually remind himself that, by law, the court exists for the people. The government exists to meet the needs of the people. Judges are not granted immunity when they violate their duty to protect the citizen's rights. Such facts help people in the network to reframe and take positive action. Being available to and supportive of victims, Tom has probably inadvertently diverted the untimely deaths of several judges.

Chapter 9

Empowerment
Your Personal Realm of Power

> *"I know how to be abased and I know how to abound."*
> Phillippians 4:12-13

Empowerment comes to LAS victims in the form of focused energy. After denial is relinquished and the trauma processed, there is a reintegration of the self. The preceding steps bring the victim to the point of being able to let go of denial, his natural protective device. Regardless of protection, denial will become the enemy by rendering the victim less potent during litigation. Hanging on to denial is simply too costly. Nor does denial protect against the lifetime of recurring reminders that will momentarily trigger LAS symptoms. The price of denying ugly reality is living life as a fugitive from the everpresent facts.

Empowerment will emanate from the reframed self only after the payment of incredible dues. The victim pays his dues by going back into rage and effectively taking ownership of his ravaged existence. Saying "I own this horror" releases the kidnapped soul. Disillusionment and denial are then replaced by a firm and courageous grasp of the facts of his predicament.

Legal abuse presents a challenge of the worst sort. The assault has been no "act of God." You've been assaulted by those people and systems that you trusted, a bad will from those you've employed and supported. It is like being methodically disemboweled with your own assets being turned on you. When you are, isolated, assaulted, virtually bound and gagged in terms of control of your properties and rights, you have nothing left to own but the horror.

Sheer guts come into play in the face of a full frontal assault when victims begin to take charge. At that moment, empowerment has begun. You are back in the game. There are no guarantees, but at least the fight becomes more difficult for the wrongdoers.

The LAS victim's alternative to ownership of the dilemma and empowerment is to remain in denial, exactly what his perpetrators want. Then he will be no "trouble" to his court, bureaucratic systems, or to those who surround him. The price he pays for compliance is relinquishment of all hope of restoration and he may go mad.

Each step in this book leads the LAS victim back into rage for a time. It is a dreaded but temporary trip back through the pain, like going through a tunnel of swords or down in a hot, crowded elevator. Debriefing and the steps that follow uproot buried rage, tempting the victim to flee. Reframing brings relief and opens a door to freedom. However, only the next step, empowerment, helps the victim, now veteran, find his realm of power propelling him forward through the open door and allowing him to shed his cellophane cocoon once and for all.

Skills for empowerment:
- Seek and Destroy Misinformation
- Form Pragmatic Expectations
- Avoid the Predictable

- Persevere if Your Principles Dictate
- Use Mental Toughness
- Become a Vigilante Consumer
- Call a Crime, a Crime

Seek and Destroy Misinformation

LAS victims are not wrestled down by laws, lack of laws, cumbersome bureaucracies or overburdened courts nearly as much as by <u>misinformation</u>. Oppression thrives on misinformation. It crushes the force of the truth and distorts the course of justice regardless of the forum.

White-collar criminals, like James' contractor, feed misinformation into the court and investigative agencies. James' contractor reported that he was owed $250,000 for overages on the job. They were mythical, but were reported again and again. He was paid the same $250,000 repeatedly from a variety of sources. All the time, James continued to produce evidence against the claim and to challenge the misinformation. The contractor had paid attorneys with moneys stolen from James. These attorneys force-fed paperwork behind the mythical $250,000 and squelched all challengers. When the contractor was exonerated by the court, due to misinformation given to the jury, the myth took on an official appearance. That court decision formed the basis for continuing the $250,000 caper. It worked once, why stop?

LAS victims believe that their empowerment lies in the truth, the evidence, appropriate procedure, and paying attorneys' fees and legal costs. As they prepare for court, the perpetrator is introducing misinformation which, as we can see, eventually grows until it takes on a life of its own. The perpetrator and his hired guns further use misinformation to mistreat and discredit the LAS victim. Slanderous misinformation justifies mistreatment of the victim. The victim finds his simple truth and fair presentation shrinking beside the mutating, mythical and entertaining prevarication. While outrage builds, he is told to remain patient and "let the system work."

The minute the LAS victim realizes that he's been had, he is greeted by oppression as part of the hostage condition. Next, the victim is oppressed by the continually generated misinformation, the prime tool of all perpetrators. Finally, he is in danger of internalizing oppression by giving up the fight. Whenever you hear someone ask, "What's the use of fighting?" or say, "You can't fight the system," they have internalized oppression. These self-oppressors have quit using their realms of power.

Oppression thrives on misinformation. We are facing a large segment of the population being invisibly oppressed as LAS victims proliferate and our courts and their judicial companion agencies are mutated by misinformation. Bastions against justice are created that hold out and reject the *pro se, pro per* litigant along with the citizens reporting crimes.

In our midst, a target group has entered the oppressive picture. It transcends civil rights for persons of color, ethnicities, genders, ages, the unborn, and the religious. It is made up of the unrecognized middle-class, *pro se* or *pro per* litigants and honest citizens discriminated against in their searches for justice. Proponents, blaming color or other factors, leave this group without recognition of the true causes of civil rights abuses. The targeted group is splintered as a result and left without advocacy. The invisible LAS victims I speak of are pummeled by systemic mistreatment as adapted from Far West Laboratory for Educational Research and Development in San Fransisco.

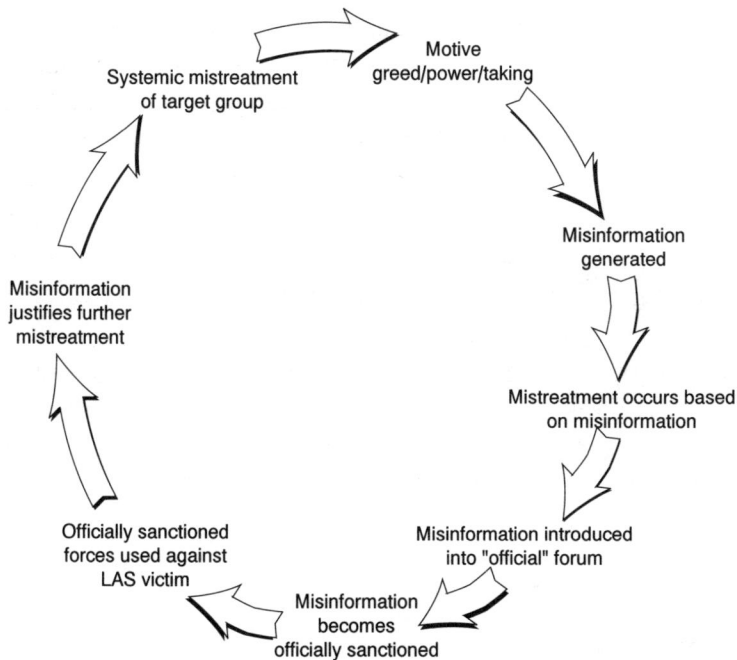

Oppressive Cycle

Birth of a mutation begins at the moment a well-intentioned investigator intakes truth and misinformation equitably. Yet the agency, its policies, or the investigator will be hard put to begin any other way. Tom, John, James, and Manny were called "disgruntled litigants," fools, crazy, and "unable to take 'no' for an answer." Profoundly influencing each of their cases were numerous documents and presentations containing misinformation. When challenged, official explanations were freely transmitted among those who enjoy titles that alluded to "authorized," "trustee" or "official." Even though the misinformation caused massive destruction to these people, it was always accepted without verification. Submissions from Tom, James, John, and Manny were deemed "unofficial." Therefore, the truth was dismissed repeatedly and without a second look. Tom found, in his case, that the clerks were instructed to dismiss any incoming paperwork from him without review.

Within every LAS victim's realm of power is knowledge of the truth. He remains the only party in a protracted legal battle who knows the truth and cares that the truth prevails. All others will not prioritize truth over efficiency, funding, expediency, or other common motivations of judicial personnel. The victim's evidence and motivations are wasted during the fact finding process.

When James was forced to pay the contractor's legal fees of $60,000 after the contractor used misinformation to be exonerated, all court personnel took the decision as official and moved on with oppressive actions. James was treated with impatience and disdain when he wanted to appeal the decision. His own attorney recognized the now "official" picture and truly had no interest in right versus wrong prevailing. There had been no way for James' impeccable credibility to be contrasted with the contractor's 13-year history of accusations of white-collar crime and complaints to his board. The entire response (costing more than $100,000) to James' evidence was never elevated beyond a low level character assassination and name-calling session. Only the oppression from the power game of officially sanctioned lies now lives for James. The truth was dead, buried and he was urged to forget it.

An arena for truth would bring most LAS victims back from beyond rage and they would stand a fair chance in spite of an unwieldy system. No one will provide such a forum for victims. They must do it for themselves. If victims do not continue to fight back within their realms of power, oppression from misinformation is irreversible. In lieu of a formal place where truth can be valued, victims need to respond to misinformation, forcing truth through the membrane of "officiality."

Force Rapid Responses

Rapid response strategies are the key to dealing with misinformation.

1. Respond - always respond. To give up in the face of officially sanctioned misinformation, the most discouraging and common contributor to LAS, is to succumb to internalized oppression. Do not become your own oppressor.

2. Deny concisely and unequivocally any word, any element, or any attempt at placing wrongdoing or impropriety at your feet.

3. Force clarification of all misinformation in a clear, objectively stated list. Supply a list of all supporting documents.

4. State your intent to see to it that laws, rules, and regulations are carried out by the responsible parties. Use mental toughness statements to punctuate your area of focus.

5. Make your determination of how the party you are addressing is violating his own directives and your knowledge of the facts. Regardless of the titles of those who might be willing to sanction it, official capacity does not excuse misinformation becoming part of the formal record.

6. Make your demand that all misinformation be corrected by the appropriate authorities and all damage incurred to you be halted. You are to be restored to the point where the introduction of misinformation began to distort the record and subsequent actions.

7. State your authority. Quote the laws, policies, and dictates that support your demand. Further, ethics, right and wrong, morals, issues of character, and common law need to be stated and restated.

8. Request a response within a set time limit.

9. Make a back-up plan if there is no response or an unfavorable response. Always have a "worst case scenario" plan on hand.

10. Reframe your presumptions and force public servants to reframe their presumptions.

From:

(A) "If the data is presented by a licensed attorney, an official of an agency, a branch of government or personnel of the court that the data must be correct, affirmed, defended, and accepted without verification."

To:

(B) "The record must reclaim the truth if there has been an error. I am responsible to verify all reports of misinformation even if my time is short and I must place more of the burden on the victim to supply supporting data."

From:

(A) "If a victim presents information or a demand to the court or agency, he is a 'disgruntled litigant' who is unreasonable, and a 'pain in the neck' who won't settle."

To:

(B) "Victims have a huge investment in the truth being reclaimed. I owe the public respect and correction

if errors have been made."
11. Gain allies and get help. If all of this sounds like too much tedious homework, get help. Victims' empowerment is greatly enhanced when they network. Some groups are supporting one another's clarification letters. When Tom received the following outrageous responses from an "official" source, rapid response letters were sent in his behalf from other victims in California, Texas, Arizona, Florida, and New Jersey. Allies are supporters in positions of power.

The letter arrived on official stationery from the U.S. Department of Justice, Office of Professional Responsibility. As we all know, Tom was never in bankruptcy. He had a claim as a creditor in bankruptcy court. Quoted from Tom's official letter:

The letter begins:

> "This is in response to your letter to this Office in which raised (sic) your concerns regarding certain events pertaining to your bankruptcy case."

The letter goes on to list Tom's submissions to the courts providing evidence and law for the purpose of clarifying misinformation and wrongdoing in his case. The names will be omitted:

> "Upon review of your submissions, we noted

that on March 8, 1993, the United States court of appeals for the Federal Circuit affirmed a lower court's dismissal of your action. Moreover, in its decision in .....v....., the Federal circuit assessed damages of $2,000 against you because it found your appeal to be 'both frivolous as filed and frivolous as argued.'"

Sadly, the first of all of the matters was colored by the decision of a judge who was later sent to prison for wrongdoing. Yet Tom is continuing to be punitively dismissed because the misinformation now has a life of its own.

The letter concludes:

"Language in the Federal Circuit's opinion shows that you litigated the issues in an earlier 1989 Second Circuit case captioned .....v..... Indeed, in .....v....., after being cautioned by the Second circuit against bringing any further action, you apparently disregarded that court's warning and brought a subsequent appeal of the same district court action. Upon granting the appellee's motion to dismiss the subsequent appeal, the Second Circuit, finding that your arguments were without merit and that your appeal was frivolous, imposed a $1,000 (sic) in sanctions against you.
Given the foregoing, we are unable to find any evidence of misconduct on the part of either.... (sic)

in rejecting your complaint.
Moreover, in light of the decisions by both appellate courts to assess damages against you, it appears that your allegation against.....and ..... for 'clouding the issue on appeal' is also without merit.

Absent evidence of misconduct by individuals falling within the scope of our jurisdiction, we cannot consider your complaint further."

Tom got the members of the network to write, not only to the paralegal who generated this letter, but also to her superiors and Tom's congresspersons, and one member of the network provided this poorly written letter to the media. The supportive actions of the network energize Tom and his family, bolstering their ability to keep up the struggle. Each letter that was sent validated Tom and his family to those in official capacities. They were urged to investigate the misinformation in view of the fine character and credibility of these citizens. They were reminded that Tom's story was the story of many middle Americans and those in the network were watching for the outcome of Tom's case.

12. When your sanity or credibility is questioned, you need help from others. Legal abuse tactics unfortunately will often include attacking your claim to your sanity. Psychiatrists and psychologists must not be seen in a mystical light that allows them to analyze your mind. No one person can analyze anything other than what is presented to them. They have no magical key into your mind. Good

psychiatric reports must meet professional requirements the same as any other report compiled for the court (Margenau).

A. Question issues of confidentiality. Unless you sign a release of information form, confidentiality is to be respected. Further, rapport with the psychiatrist is critical to a thorough report being compiled. The report should contain:

1. The purpose of the examination including documentation of the patient's understanding of the purpose of the examination
2. Consent by the patient to being examined
3. Time and place of the examination and under what circumstances the patient has been seen
4. Conclusions
5. Personal history
6. Psychiatric history
7. Surrounding circumstances or the patient's involvement with the legal issues or situation
8. Results of mental status examination and psychological testing
9. Diagnosis

B. The report should be extremely accurate regarding pertinent data in the form of a summary. Psychiatric symptoms, problems and impairments are to be discussed <u>without</u> going into detailed discussion of psychodynamic factors.

Sandy was forced to succumb to psychiatric testing as part of her litigation experience. Opposing counsel set up the psychiatric session. When Sandy arrived, she was angry, threatened, and distrustful. The doctor was late for their appointment which kept her waiting and further agitated her. They met for two hours.

She was shocked when she received, after arduous effort, a copy of her psychiatric report. It opened, stating that it was a report of an "...extended, two part, four session psychiatric evaluation interview which consumed the entire morning of April 30, 1993." The above subjectively rather than objectively describes the time, place, and length of the session. She immediately feared the report because the time had been misrepresented at the outset.

Next a warning in bold capital letters preceded the report. It warned that the report was not to be shown to Sandy. Confidential reports usually carry a warning that they are confidential and to be read by the intended parties only. The wording, "EXPERIENCE SHOWS THAT PEOPLE READING THEIR OWN REPORTS DEVELOP DISTORTED, VERY THREATENING MISUNDERSTANDINGS, WHICH HARM THE READERS. ANY PERSON IGNORING THIS AUTOMATICALLY ASSUMES RESPONSIBILITY FOR DAMAGE TO THE PATIENT," glared at her from the front page of the report. It intimidated any person that allowed Sandy to see it and did not warn of broadly sharing the confidential information.

Sandy felt terribly alone and frightened as she read a report that discredited her ability to testify in her own behalf. Quoted from the report:

> "...we are about to see that many of Sandy's ways of responding to questions and making statements during the interview gave consistent evidence that she is not a credible medical-psychiatric historian."

As a mental health professional, I write many reports for the court. The importance of a conservative approach to discrediting any witness, including the adversary of my patient, cannot be over emphasized. Further, a frightened, hostile client will answer in a frightened, hostile manner. It is the job of the examiner to either establish rapport or report fairly that it could not be established.

The examiner's statements about Sandy: ("...pausing before answering, making exaggerated statements, remembering a sudden onset of problems, speaking in hostile terms, inconsistent memory in dealing with her attorney") were used as the bases for his psychiatric conclusions. No objective tests were performed.

Never once did the psychiatrist, with a long list of credentials, take into account Sandy's victimization. She had lost her half of a computer business to a partner who schemed with the company attorney. The attorney had represented the business and had her trust. She turned to the court and found herself an LAS victim facing false accusations of mismanagement and other damning misinformation. She has continued to fight and now her sanity is being exploited against her in the court.

Form Pragmatic Expectations

We left Tom and his family in a legal mire that seems impossible to own and manage. Yet, through understanding the scope of rules, regulations, and laws confronting him, Tom set expectations that were manageable within his realm of power. Tom took ownership of the following predicament:

1. The seller demanded immediate payment of rents 154% over the agreed upon amount.

2. The seller demanded $2,000 attorneys' fees for clearing the title.

3. The seller returned all certified checks for agreed upon rents and sued the family.

4. The property was foreclosed upon by the original mortgage holder.

5. Tom had spent $13,000 in legal fees at this point and had sustained 2 1/2 years of psycholegal trauma.

6. A sheriff's car drove into their front yard and served notice of a $20,000 attachment. The attach-

ment was filled with slander and what Tom calls "vile allegations." They went to court.

7. They were out of money after the first court case. They faced months of interrogatories, motions, and counter motions.

8. During a deposition the seller admitted that he and his Connecticut attorney had never intended to sell the property to Tom. He wanted to use Tom's resources to enhance the value of the property and then sell it after they were forced out. The family was relieved when they found out that the bankruptcy had moved from a chapter 11 to chapter 7 and now a trustee was in charge of the property. A trustee had to abide by a strict code of ethics and rules that would protect Tom and his family.

9. Tom obtained a jury trial which heard the case against the sellers. The jury found that Tom had been induced into a fraud and awarded him $52,000.

10. Tom filed to collect the award.

11. The Judge refused to allow collection of the award stating that there were no assets in the estate. Tom knew better.

12. Tom contacted the trustee and asked that he facilitate the payment of the jury award.

13. The trustee's attorney wrote to the family informing them that the trustee did not intend to pay. Further, if Tom attempted to collect, that he would be sanctioned from the Federal Bankruptcy Court.

14. Tom filed to collect. Every effort was frustrated and many laws and procedures violated. Finally, the California Bankruptcy Court issued an order enjoining Tom from executing judgment against the trustee.

15. Tom appealed because the California Bankruptcy Court did not have jurisdiction over the Connecticut State Court jury judgment.

16. Tom and his family suffered financial collapse.

17. Tom was diagnosed with a hernia and needed surgery. He had no financial ability to obtain surgery.

18. A news story broke. The trustee had been indicted for bankruptcy violations. He entered a plea agreement with the U.S. Attorney's Office in which he admitted embezzling in excess of $2 million from two estates (the figure later was found to be more

like $5 million). He was sentenced to 2 years imprisonment at a federal facility of his choice (Club Fed), ordered to make restitution, and fined $5,000. Further investigation showed his unlawful takings were up to $40,000,000.

19. Tom became aware that he had been the victim of a massive racketeering enterprise.

20. In 1989, Tom filed a legal document including two claims of civil racketeering against the judges in his case. This complaint named the six federal officers and court appointed agents who controlled the bankruptcy. Judges were named due to their unlawful exercise of federal powers.

21. In 1990, his complaint was dismissed amidst a shower of intimidating dialogue from the presiding judge. Legal authority was not challenged, just ignored by the judge. Tom did his legal work with little help from lawyers. Attorneys who have looked at his work comment that he is meticulous in his adherence to the truth and to the authority that is within strict bounds of the letter and intent of the law.

Had Tom approached his court matter purely idealistically, he could have contributed to his own frustration. Instead, he remained patient, and adjusted his expectations, allowing him to act within his realm of truth. He entered court acting as his own attorney, *pro se*. Regardless of Constitutional and legal authority as a *pro se* litigant, he was treated like the nonmember of an exclusive club. In the unpopular and frightening posture of a *pro se* litigant, Tom learned that adherence to court procedure and case preparation must be impeccable. Even so, the lips of opposing counsel will sneer in ridicule attempting to debase the morale of those who will seek their rights without an attorney.

Tom's realm of empowerment emerges from his leadership ability coupled with his newly centered self. Tom studied. He knows what the laws provide. He also is well grounded in reality. His system, so far, has ignored the laws that protect him and has oppressed him due to misinformation. Without the foundation he has gained from his studies and realistic expectations confidently set, he would be easily bluffed out of court.

Instead, Tom, through conviction, intelligence, and leadership, has brought his case all the way to the United States Supreme Court. He is confident about arguing his case on the floor of the Supreme Court if he is allowed. All of this from a citizen who was defiled by his system and who grew taller than the wrongs.

Avoid the Predictable

When you're in litigation, lawyers know that information will be obtained through subpoenas, interrogatories, and depositions. The polished perpetrator will have a thousand ways of manipulating that data. Study your opposition. Do not allow yourself to be put in a defensive posture. Gather information like a reporter and approach the task like an undercover investigator. Do your own research or use research from a network of similar cases, including laws that have been used effectively.[6]

---

6. Networking sources and empowering referral resources are listed in Appendix B.

Tools and techniques your perpetrator won't expect:

1. Learn to use the Freedom of Information Act, 5 U.S.C. 552.[7] If the organization serves the public, you're entitled to the information as long as you use the correct form.

2. Learn to appreciate and use your law librarian. They are usually untapped sources of information and can be immensely helpful and knowledgeable. Use your law library.

3. Use your courts even if you can't afford a lawyer. It is no longer true if you appear in court *pro se* that you have a "fool for a client." A growing number of resources are available for those who must use court in *propria persona* or act as their own attorney.

4. If you want to study or report white-collar crime, order Jane Y. Kusic's book *White Collar Crime 101*. It will give you the proper channels for complaint and recourse. Jane Y. Kusic's organization is excellent for first-step reporting.

5. After you have the proper channels for recourse that are listed in Jane Kusic's book, get ready for frustration and keep *Legal Abuse Syndrome - Beyond Rage...and Back* handy. Remember, the per-

---

[7]. Exact text of the Freedom of Information Act is quoted in Appendix C along with a sample request letter and letter of appeal.

petrator may have introduced misinformation influencing the standard channels for recourse ahead of you and made alliances to ward off complaints.

6. Start your own grass roots organization or join others and empower their efforts. You are not alone. The skills and strengths you need are available through networking.

7. Contact powerful people who demonstrate principle. Form alliances. Addresses for contacting famous people with clout can be found in the reference section of the public library.

8. Don't just write your Congresspeople. Remember, that is predictable. Find a forum where they are speaking and make a statement designed to arouse applause from the audience. Politicians always note which statements received applause.

9. Don't accept your Congresspersons telling you that they cannot intervene in your behalf with judicial matters because the branches of government must remain separate. Spelled out in the House Ethics Manual are the Congresspersons' duties. They are to function as a "go-between" or conduit between constituents and administrative agencies of the Federal Government and the courts.

10. Use or start a "court support" group. These groups differ from court watching. The group forms a telephone chain to keep in touch with one another's court dates and progress. When a member goes to court, the other members go with him in support. The rules are clear that absolute appropriate court behavior is followed: no radical activities are allowed. The court room fills with comforting and supportive citizens to witness, firsthand, the court in action. Written support can be provided in the form of a brief, an Amicus Curiae, filed as a neutral friend of the court in behalf of the case.

11. Study the detailed policies and practices of your opponent's agency, corporation, or company. Often victims find that perpetrators have violated their own dictates and rules. The infrastructure of victims' empowerment lies in creative channels to information and action. Conscience-centered people suffering from shame and abuse are susceptible to attack. They are easily caught up in defensive actions rather than aggressive counter-moves. Hostages do not easily think of studying their opposition nor of challenging those who appear to "run the show." Tom spent nine years defending his position, complying with court requirements, and submitting to demands of opposing counsel. Finally, he realized the organized

wrongdoings that he had faced. Tom is now in an aggressive posture. Regardless of attempts to dismiss him, Tom respectfully and appropriately approaches his court again and again according to law.

Persevere

Delays, dismissals, unhelpful responses, diversions, expenses, inefficiencies, and red-tape function to force a victim to throw up his hands, give up, and go away. Abusers and their appointees, through tactical manipulations, block the LAS victim at every turn. It will feel like an entire system is conspiring, in concert, to drive the litigant to irrationality.

Chloe's handsome and charming husband used all of the above maneuvers as a matter of course. He was a prominent businessman who worked on maintaining contacts with those in political power. Accustomed to getting what he wanted with a phone call, when challenged, he simply wore down his opponent with legal and emotional intrigue. He firmly believed that Chloe, who lived a sheltered life, would be easy to "leave in the dust." She was always mesmerized by his cunning style. Chloe had a surprise for her soon-to-be-former husband.

The Story of Chloe

It was an unusual bedtime in Chloe's home. After dinner, her husband had informed her that he had filed for divorce and he would be moving out the next day. He also advised her that he was using the most powerful law firm in the state. If she intended to retain any other substantial firm, it would be to no avail since he had had dealings with them all. They would not represent any client opposing him. She would get a subsistence survival settlement. She was told that she would be lucky to get anything and to accept his divorce proposal basically giving him the estate worth $1,200,000.

Before the divorce, she describes her life with him as "no picnic." He deliberately schemed to burden her with responsibilities and duties, and induced problems that regularly overwhelmed her. She realized that he was an artist in creating confusion and then manipulating her while she lacked clarity of thought. But, he was the father of her children and provided for his family.

Chloe told of living as a hostage unaware. Nevertheless, she believed that she had a fighting chance if given her fair day in court. She would not easily be intimidated.

Single parenting of four children did not frighten her if they were provided for. Chloe's mother had also been a single parent. As a child she had found many ways to cope with the world without masculine power in her life.

Chloe refused to relinquish her power or to be subordinated regardless of the fact that her ex-husband, as a gambling executive, was a man with connections to the top of the political hierarchy. Every time Chloe faced her ex-husband in court, she was defeated. Cronyism and the "good old boy" network wiped her out. Opposing counsel confidently applied methods of delay to frustrate her. She found herself dismissed from court and abandoned by one attorney after another for 15 years.

Her oldest child graduated from high school. She could not afford graduation pictures or to send her on her senior trip. Chloe sat at graduation, with her three younger children, having to decide between sure poverty or continuing to fight alone.

She describes her belief system as focused on fairness. She had always been an independent thinker in the midst of an economically dependent lifestyle as a homemaker and mother of four children. Chloe fought her legal battle because she knew it was the right thing for her to do.

When Chloe contacted me, long after the graduation, she began by stating, "My life is utter chaos. I have lost control and all I do is wait. We have yet to receive the opinion of the judge." Working the legal process by retarding progress is especially brutal on ordinary people like Chloe. She went on, "It's impossible to invest in any new and satisfying direction. Their goal is to reduce me to a level of poverty and despair in order to force me to discontinue this battle of wills."

Chloe began to take each lawyer who had violated his ethical responsibilities before the regulating board. She won small settlements from three different lawyers. The small wins energized her and she began to use the funds toward her quest for a fair settlement again. It was tough enough that the children were abandoned by their father. All the while, her ex-husband lived an ostentatiously extravagant lifestyle with little regard for his family. He paid only what he was forced to pay, at the last moment. This economic disparity infuriated Chloe. She was determined that economic abandonment would not stand.

"I consider myself to be resilient; however, there are times when doubt takes over. I'm very aware that my children's future is dependent on me as a consequence of the betrayal of their father," she stated. "The burden of fighting the legal system alone is a lifestyle by now. I see that the moves of my adversaries are subtle and seemingly without end. It's the chase that holds the interest for my ex-husband and his gang of attorneys who will abuse and violate the system in his behalf."

Chloe is caught where many LAS victims find themselves. She's not willing to compromise on principles that are paramount to the heritage of her family. Tenacity feels instinctive. The weaponry of the psychopath no longer deters her. Chloe's ability to persevere is nourished by her sense of responsibility and thoughtful concern about her dilemma and its implications beyond herself.

> "My life's work seems to have more than one purpose: I must be true to myself and live by my principles, and, however small the mark, to provide for my family and contribute to a better world."

Chloe's tenacity finally paid off. She left a message that she "won and won big." At this point Chloe has persevered in the courts for <u>15 years</u>. Her children are grown, never having known a normal childhood without the ongoing court battle. Her grandchildren have inherited the legacy of a third generation facing the same court case. Some people call Chloe "crazy" and others find her forbidding in her continuing effort to gain legally and rightfully what is due. I can't help but admire this person who stands for right versus wrong and models it for her posterity. She certainly has presented her husband with the challenge of his life. He is assured that she will not fold under pressure. The price that Chloe has paid is tremendous.

I wonder what this intelligent and insightful person may have contributed to our society if her time and energy had been freed by the court through a timely decision a decade ago. Justice continues to be denied through delays, even though Chloe finally won in court. Chloe summarized:

> "I'm rather depleted at this point. This war has been going on for more than four decades and the divorce did not remedy the problem, it merely compounded it. Domestic struggle of this kind appears to go on until death or demise by a principle party. If my ex-husband were to come to terms with the far reaching effects of his actions and

omissions, I have to believe that living would be too difficult for him to sustain."

Use Mental Toughness

Mental toughness is a term used in sports. Toughness of the mind relates to the ability to concentrate and execute a planned performance under difficult conditions. The ability to envision yourself and your desired result is fundamental to this concept (Loehr).

Victims rehearse and picture themselves presenting their cases in court. They practice anger control, check their self esteem, and improve their visualization skills by using three fundamental principles:

1. I visualize only myself and the performance that I can control.

2. I will not engage when the adversary is trying to make me angry or lose control.

3. I will be prepared and I will perform without losing focus on my goal.

Power-centered adversaries rarely respond to legal charges; instead, they divert attention or attack the victim. If they do not want to deal with the issue, regulators and bureaucrats have pat answers to put off the action or to negate it. Victims commonly report that regulators, upon being presented with a complaint, present forms to be filled out. They readily inform the victim of his rights. After the forms are completed, the agency will accept the complaint and then request a response from the offender. If the offender is using power tactics, he will respond with diversionary comments and misinformation. The agency then informs the victim of the offender's "position."

Having informed the complainant of the offender's response, civil action might be recommended, at which point the bureaucrat then files all copies after informing the complainant of the response. The PC is greatly aided by this cycle of agencies "guarding their own backs" and putting little effort into fact finding or righting a wrong. Smoothing over, slipping away after a neutral inquiry, does not satisfy the taxpayer who needs protective regulation firmly enforced.

Mental toughness is staying tough in your mind and, regardless of emotions or hurdles thrown in your way, being able to execute your goals:

1. Muster your authority. By now you are empowered with the laws designed to protect you and the foundation from which they spring. Have them on hand and be able to quote the laws verbally or in writing.

2. Your empowerment contains knowledge of the rules, procedures, and parameters of the organization you're approaching. You are even able to quote from their procedure manuals.

3. Approach the organization with preparation and perseverance. Tell them exactly what you want done and when.

4. As the authority, keep all parties on focus by shifting gears between asserting authority and hearing opposing responses. After listening, reflecting your understanding, and acknowledging the other's position, reassert your demand and authority.

When the focus begins to be diverted from your goal use:

"Nevertheless"
"Regardless"
"Nonetheless"
"Notwithstanding"
"It doesn't matter"

After the diversionary statement is made, use the following in order to begin restating the other's position:

"I hear you"
"I understand"
"It sounds like"
"Yes"
"From your point of view"

Then, by turning the conversation back with the lead-ins above, restate your authority and your demand forcing the focus back to your point.

James had an encounter with the IRS after he was billed improperly for a tenant's taxes. After a series of outrageous responses and James supplying the laws and evidence to show clearly that it was not his bill, he asked to speak to the Ombudsman, hoping that someone might bring reason into the dispute. The Ombudsman was a young man who listened while James presented the frustrating and inaccurate correspondence received from the IRS. Soon it became apparent that the Ombudsman was going to rationalize misinformation and inaccurate responses. James vowed to be mentally tough.

O: "Mr....you are being penalized for refusing to pay the tax in a timely manner."

J: "Yes, the IRS is under the wrong assumption that I had access to the funds of this company and responsibility to pay. You see by the signature card from the bank and the officers in the corporation that I had no way to know that the tax was owed, no responsibility to pay it, and no access to the funds of the company."

O: "Somehow they got your name as being responsible to pay."

J: "Yes, you can see that there has been a mistake. Since I did not know they were owed and couldn't write a check on their account, it would have been impossible for me to pay. How can the IRS find that the impossible is possible?"

O: "They must have a good reason. You had a hearing and you were found responsible to pay."

J: "Nevertheless, the law states that I am not a 'person' in the eyes of the law as it relates to paying taxes, according to ....v....."

O: "Well, you'll have to pay it and then you file a claim to get it back."

J: "I understand that is your preferred procedure; regardless, I do not owe it and do not choose to pay what I do not owe."

5. Be prepared for diversionary tactics. You will never be able to anticipate the breadth and depth of outrageous spew that will emerge at an adversarial proceeding.

Without general preparation for any diversionary move, a victim will be caught off guard. The adversaries' goal is to frustrate the victim out of action or to divert until the matters argued do not accomplish the victim's objectives (Bodenhamer).

Become A Vigilante Consumer

Tough consumers demand their civil rights including fair and safe courts. Officials of a public service must be forced to serve the public. Consumers assume that their courts are financed by tax dollars in order to offer the public a civilized, legal forum for the resolution of their disputes. Yet they've become privatized to the extent that, without an ABA attorney in court, a fair result is rare.

Consider public schools with their obligation to educate all children regardless of economic status, academic ability, or handicap. What if the public schools performed their duties like the public courts, both financed by tax dollars? Think of a school that you could not effectively enter unless you privately retained a teacher and administrator who belonged to a certified professional organization. An "American Education Association" would operate like the American Bar Association. All children could come to the school, sit at the desks, and hold the books; however, tutelage would only be granted to those who could pay their teacher of record. We would soon have education only for the privileged.

Vigilante consumers must demand their civil rights and a true value for their tax dollars from their public service systems. The vigilante consumer of the future will neither take a brush-off or a <u>no</u> for an answer nor will he "shoot the messenger," the innocent worker who provides the public contact for the organization. He will steadfastly work to empower himself and to address the abuses of power that infiltrate systems as a matter of human failing. His steady force will make a difference in correcting the systemic frailties created by the power-centered.

Call Crime a Crime

Tom had to see through the veil of legalese in order to identify that a federal judge was committing a crime. The judge didn't fit the stereotype of a criminal and the setting felt orderly and official. It was, after all, the place that Tom had turned for justice. Yet, while doubting his own sanity, Tom had to face that a crime was being committed and then he had to have the courage to step up and take legal action against the judge.

Kropatkin presents an equation for the enablement of crime:

TARGET + MOTIVE + ACCESS + OPPORTUNITY = A CRIMINAL ATTACK

White-collar crime is described as:

> Wrongful activity or some aspect of a wrongful pattern of activity committed by the use of misrepresentation, guile, or deception (nonphysical means) to obtain something of value, prevent loss, or obtain personal or business advantage, and often in violation of a fiduciary relationship (Kropatkin).

When we consider takings, as opposed to blatant robbery, it is easy to see that the clever, legalized takings by abusers of the system are plainly crime. Let's call the crime, *crime*. Even though it may be easy, profitable, cute, a badge to be worn among the unethical legal community, or seemingly invisible to the average observer, it's a crime.

Opposite from the well-intentioned investigator formerly described, there will be champions of agencies who will hear no wrong of the systems. Thus, a problem reported by some victims is in attempting to expose the crimes. Their attempts are extinguished by the first overzealous and protective investigator that they approach. When Tom reported the crime, the person he alerted in authority was such a type. He queried in response to Tom's evidence, "Surely, you are not implying that officers of the court are involved in crime?" And, when James reported to the FBI, he was told that the judge was a wonderful person and a neighbor of the agent and certainly would not be involved in any wrongdoing. Sandy reported crime to the FBI and was told that she was accusing one of the largest law firms in the state of California of violations and must be mistaken. So, these self appointed front line judge/jury/executioner-types literally quash any ability to correct or to expose the crime running rampant in our society.

Crime needs to be confronted where it happens regardless of the pious trappings that may surround the perpetrator. We may want efforts at justice to be blind, but not blind, deaf, and dumb. We must call crime a crime and take action to thwart it.

> Tom reframed his attitude from "The Constitution empowers us," to a more narrow interpretation, "The Constitution is the charter by which 'we, the people,' govern ourselves." Tom represented himself in court. After Tom had endured the painful rigors of two weeks in court, lies, distortions, tricks, and misinformation, the jury saw through it all and found in his favor. That moment was a monumental, empowering experience.

The judge then arbitrarily chose to enjoin Tom from receiving the award of the jury. At that point Tom vowed to fight to the end. According to Tom, this was necessary in the face of tyranny, and he quoted the fourteenth Amendment, "nor shall any State deprive any person of life, liberty, or property, without due process of law; nor deny to any person within its jurisdiction the equal protection of the laws." If the government does not do its job, the citizen must take over on behalf of the government.

A basic course in civics, perhaps, but it looms into giant perspective for John, James, and Tom, all veterans of war. Now they are all veterans of victimization by their own system. They agree that judges and attorneys are violating the victim protection law as much, or more than, the common criminal. Although witnesses must take the oath "...to tell the truth, the whole truth, and nothing but the truth," in each of the cases cited above the oath was intentionally violated by attorneys getting fair evidence withheld, badgering, and slandering witnesses, and purposefully misleading the court. We have been told that:

> "We must tolerate a little extra crime in America in order to preserve our civil liberties." Tucker states that this idea is nonsense. The right to be relatively safe and secure in your home and on the street is just as much a civil liberty as the right to a grand jury indictment or a fair trial. And the right to choose between degrees of safety and security on the one

hand, and extreme civil libertarianism, on the other, is an even more basic right of a free people (Tucker).

The invisible crimes, the kinds of crimes we have talked about in this book, lack entertainment value for the nightly news. They are minimized. When a violent crime is portrayed on television, the injury is indisputable and the injurer can be easily identified. Crimes created out of deceptions and misinformation cannot be communicated in a picture or a sound byte. They are laborious, expensive, and tedious to resolve and sometimes nearly impossible to perceive.

Victims need a clearly defined role in criminal justice proceedings, beginning with following 18 USC Sec. 4., which states that when a citizen has knowledge of a crime he is to report it to the proper authorities. Next, regarding invisible crimes, only the victim knows every move, every detail, and is the only one who can unravel the tangled trail of misinformation that has been laid down by the perpetrators. He has to become an integral part of the investigative procedure. Justice Sandra Day O'Connor stated, "The public has just as many rights in the outcome of a criminal proceeding as does the criminal, and law enforcement is not just a confrontation between the individual and the state." I would add to Justice O'Connor's statement that victims also have a responsibility to follow their natural motivation toward justice. It may be thought crime victims have no rights because nothing is enumerated in the Constitution. The framers of the Constitution did not specify the right of crime victims to be treated fairly by the justice system. To mention the rights of victims is tantamount to reminding a citizen to go to bed or to eat meals. It was not defined because it was obvious. Only through willful neglect of the 'Founding Fathers' design does the public now need protection from its own judiciary, allowing man to be the master of himself, his destiny, and property (Tucker).

Laws are on the books for victim protection. Victim/witness assistance units were established by the Victim and Witness Protection Act of 1982 (Appendix C). Subsequently, the Office of Justice Programs was established by the Justice Assistance Act of 1984. There are five offices under the auspices of the Assistant Attorney General for the Office of Justice Programs to achieve the following:

1. Improved treatment during the judicial process.

2. Financial compensation for victims.

3. Justice system reforms to enhance truth during litigation.

It is widely assumed that these laws pertain to victims of violent crimes. However, if they are carefully read, they address all victims, including the invisible victims who suffer from LAS. LAS victims coming forth, bringing their diverse realms of power forward, will greatly help to round out the judicial picture by finally recognizing the invisible crime and the needs of its victims.

Your Realm of Power

For the trusting and trustworthy person, empowerment is an overwhelming job of micro-management of the skills outlined in this book. Invisible victims recovering from LAS, with their decency and consciences, will probably never wield political power. Tom does not expect to change his judiciary dramatically or to bring down "Goliath" with his research. Rather, his realm of empowerment contributes steadily to his values and his cherished beliefs.

LAS victims will probably not demonstrate thousands strong in the streets nor lobby as powerfully as other groups. They seem, when they're empowered, to bring forth individual creativity, unique contributions, and intelligence to an endeavor. Those who network, sharing data from their cases, do not weave a tightly woven fabric for change. They crochet it. Their empowerment comes together like a piece of lace, delicately. Individuals pulling together in loose association, bound by their common values and not wasted by soul murder, come together with enveloping strength. Like a giant lace cloth, their personal realms of power unite independent entities and catch the unaware in their expanding mesh.

Chapter 10

Recovery

The Final Step, Skilled Healing Woven Throughout Life's Journey

Trust is the pacemaker variable in group growth. From it stem all the other significant variables of health. That is to the extent that trust develops, people are able to communicate genuine feelings and perceptions of relevant issues to all members of the system.
(Gibb)

Recovery As a Life Process

Recovery is an exclusive road reserved for the brave who have faced and processed their pain. Debriefing was the first step. Recovery is the last step, which becomes a life-style of skilled problem solving. The veteran now meets and solves problems with honed wisdom, courage, and tools.

The effective veteran of LAS internalizes the process outlined in this book, interweaving the steps into his daily activities on an "as-needed" basis. When faced with trauma, the veteran automatically debriefs, identifies his losses and feelings, and recognizes areas of destabilization in his belief system. He knows for what and why he grieves. He welcomes normal tears. Blaming actions are sought. They bring justice and reinforcement of the moral code to his world. Any sense of shame is reframed into affirming appraisals that support the victim's self esteem. Obsessions are not frightening. He uses them to feed accomplishment. His realm of empowerment allows him to realistically reenter life's game. Wisdom is his companion and confidence emanates from knowledge of self and personal strength. Spiritual power flourishes.

We will revisit LAS victims whose stories were shared earlier. You will see that each person feels in command, within his realm of power, on his recovery road. Yet not one has achieved a massive victory or complete, satisfying closure. Rather, they have taken ownership of their skills, strengths, and predicaments, releasing their kidnapped souls. Recovery begins when this hostage relationship ends. There has been healing of the victim prior to a cure for the systems and perpetrators that have caused their traumas.

Ideally, this would be the point whereby the perpetrator has been confronted, forgiven, and welcomed back into society because he has learned his moral lesson. Sadly, that will be a rare occurrence. The perpetrator is usually gone or difficult to identify or is unwilling to apologize and change his ways. Recovery is left to empowerment skills used repeatedly and firmly. Tit for tat rapid responses and blaming actions must take the place of formal correction.

Recovery and Forgiveness

Recovery and Forgiveness are two entirely different things. Recovery allows the veteran of wrongdoing to affirm himself and reenter the game of life. He will win again, lose again; consequently, risk is bearable because he has coping skills with which to greet his next assault. He also constructs his life with pro-active measures to protect him and to shield his assets. Forgiveness is a personal issue to be determined by the victim. Forgiveness belongs only to the victim. Forgiveness is <u>not</u> a prerequisite for recovery.

A South African playwright, Athel Fugard, dramatizes in his stage play, *Playland*, forgiveness between one White man and one Black man. The encounter is socially profound. It is eyeball to eyeball and face to face. It is a conflict between two individuals who wrestle with social histories of collisions and atrocities. These two sinewy figures portray rugged forgiveness in a one-on-one encounter involving deep emotion and, finally, choice. Victims can never be required to let go or forgive; they must choose to forgive.

Recovery and Restoration

Forgiveness is not expected to be restorative. Restoration is separate from recovery and forgiveness. Restoration means getting back what was wrongfully taken or its equivalent. Society cannot forgive for an individual; however, it can significantly aid in their restoration. Restitution and victim's services are an important part of restoration. Any organization aimed at justice or any governmental agency responsible for serving the populace is obligated to restore LAS victims.

Each LAS veteran needs to press for restoration within his realm of power. Organize any potency you possess toward gaining your restoration. Within every victim's realm of power is the ability to advocate expanded restorative services. The Small Business Administration and other services need to explore low interest loans. LAS victims deserve disaster loans of sorts. A sensitive and closer analysis of worthiness for credit needs to bypass usual credit reports. Instead of perpetuating misinformation through manipulated credit history, governmental agencies should establish a process based on a thorough, personal check on a person's character and work history. Legal services need to be made available in an effective way for those who are left without legal representation to fight their court battles. LAS veterans, as experts in invisible crimes, need to insist that they become part of the justice process. Their contributions will aid in investigations, force perspective regarding punishment and sentencing, save dollars through volunteer efforts, and, ultimately, will eat away at the glamour and success of unchecked white-collar crime. If Tom is restored, James, John, P.J., and the others have an open door to their restoration because the legal system will have worked.

Keep the concept of restoration isolated to business. Leave emotion to the forgiveness and other recovery tasks. De-emotionalize. Compartmentalize weekly time to address restoration. Empower yourself every way you can. Continue to seek restoration. Know what you've lost and what you'll accept in order to be restored. Use every empowering device within your realm.

James could not compartmentalize a time for the business of restoration when he was in emotional denial. James was numb, frozen in time, and consumed in a deepening sense of terror when he left his beautiful home for the last time. He couldn't think for many years about getting his home back or being restored in any sense. A subsistence level of life took over. Food, shelter and transportation for himself and his family, and shielding himself from the barrage of legal demands, suffocated any thought process. That was ten years ago. James' recovery now allows him to go back to a traumatic experience with management skills rather than emotional reactions. Whenever James chooses to address his restoration, he extracts one-by-one that which he <u>can control</u> from his debriefing experience. He separates out familiar, painful feelings of rage, loss, and fear, preparing for the next contest like an athlete who uses mental toughness to greet a physical challenge. He separates his emotions from the tasks of restoration using unending mental toughness skills. He reminds himself to stay on focus. If he feels overwhelmed, he gets help or rests and gains objectivity.

Recovery, Freedom From Oppression

Whenever you make a choice, you are overcoming oppression. James chose not to continue his court battle for a certain time period. He decided that his chances of winning were slim until he had further empowered himself. He made the choice at one point to put the matter on hold until he could be postured with more strength. In the meantime, he took the evidence proving the contractor's fraud again to the District Attorney's office. After a month, he caught himself in a moment of self-oppression, saying, "They're not going to investigate. No bureaucrat does the job. No wonder crime is out of control." James was spiraling downward into a mood of "world sucks." With disgust he called to arrange the pickup of the evidence. Ironically, he was informed that it was being forwarded to a fraud unit for investigation. If the contractor is indicted, it empowers James' case and postures it to be effectively reopened.

Recovery and A Parting Look At Our Stories

James continues to move ahead while putting his legal fight to force the judge to make a decision on hold. As he and his family struggle for economic survival, his bankruptcy estate trust account has more than $100,000 excess sitting in it. He noticed that the bankruptcy trustee's attorney has regularly drawn from it and is charging the estate $90.00 per hour for the preparation of the bill that he submits. Outrage continues and James' ability to process it becomes more skilled. James shares parting words:

> "I'm a person with deep pride in my integrity and character. The emotional pain of living like a fugitive in a house that my relative has to sign for and drive a car that is not in my name and not to be able to provide a video club membership for my family or a credit card hurts. I was a provider, now I'm dependent and forced to lie to live. I don't feel shame any longer, I feel indignant.
>
> I know I'm recovering when I have surges of creativity again and yearn to build energy efficient, earthen housing. I feel cautiously able to invest in the future.
>
> Every dream has been crushed in the last 10 years. I also know that I'm not smart enough or evil enough to anticipate all power moves and trickery as I move forward.
>
> Now, I have to operate with full knowledge that I'm not protected by the judicial system of government. I'm on my own to construct my next project without being as vulnerable. I'm finding ways to construct my business life without revealing everything I own, which would jeopardize my assets in the future. I'll never own property in joint-tenancy again. That was a big mistake.
>
> Risk is the province of the businessman. Losses are part of the entrepreneur's game. I thought it was

possible to pursue happiness through business because we live in a society that purportedly provides a protective shield against abuse of power. My pursuit of happiness involves business growth. Now I know that I must prevent a need for such protection as much as possible.

My life is no longer on hold until I get a decision from the court. I am getting on with plans to develop a nonprofit service for environmentally sound building supplies and plans. I have deep concern for the nation that I'm leaving to my children. I will vote and involve myself in elections because it is within my realm of power to do so. I used to think that if I couldn't make a big difference there was no use trying. Now, I see that my inputs exercise my realm of power. Joined with others, maybe I can help. I think I'm becoming that "pain in the ass" with an eternally good attitude who those in power hate to see coming, pointing out misinformation and misdeeds in high places. I'm beginning to get some attention. Ten years of effort and I'm just scratching the surface. I'm not even close to being restored. It shouldn't take this great a toll on citizens to exercise their guaranteed rights."

Tom

"The problem is not a conflict between being ethical or getting what you want. It is being ethical <u>and</u> getting what you want. The Founding Fathers set up the Constitution to allow the pursuit of happiness while keeping in check the human weaknesses of greed and desire for power.

If the court had followed the law as it was intended, our family's financial collapse could not have happened. Society absorbs the more than $200,000,000,000 per year that is estimated to be ripped off from American citizens by white-collar crimes. With new technologies, the estimates of potential sophisticated scams are overwhelming.

I go into court alone and always over-prepared because I know that pro se cases aren't usual or appreciated by the legal brotherhood. I expect punitive treatment and know that I have to do my research and have my paperwork done well.

I have been enjoined from entering the court again. I have been sanctioned $50,000 (that means that the judge ordered that I had to pay the court $50,000 or the case could not proceed). I have had my sanity questioned and my thorough legal work dismissed for no lawful reason. I find the behavior of such judges nothing less than treasonous. I can't think of any behavior that jeopardizes our system of government more. Selling secrets to the enemy cannot damage our country any more than selling out our own citizens and constitution for quick profit.

Being a Black man, I see a different type of

division in our society now. Race, color, religion, wealth, or lack of it, are not significant divisive elements. Those Americans who abuse their power and take from the well-being and health of the nation are plainly divided against those who provide for and protect the quality of our lives. Any controversial issue is suspect in my mind. I believe that abortion, race, and other top newsworthy items are put forth to keep us from seeing the division that threatens all of us, those who abuse their powers versus those who handle power responsibly.

I've been resilient. My kids and wife have gone through hell. I never expected my government to solve my problems. I also don't expect it to create problems and then, foursquare, stand in the way of the solutions or violate the citizens of this country and their rights to due process and redress.

I guess recovery for me has amounted to knowing who I am and what I stand for. I've been tested. I'm a man with conviction. I will not give up. If I have the opportunity, I know that I can present my case on the floor of the Supreme Court of the United States. I call that being healed in spite of the odds against me."

Tom currently has a petition filed with the U.S. Supreme Court regarding right to due process and right to redress; excerpts can be found in Appendix B.

P.J.

"I'm still in a daily wrestling match with reality. I'm permanently disabled from my spinal cancer and have been forced into early retirement. My family punishes me for holding my criminal relative accountable. The bureaucracies that I've appealed to punish me for asking them to do their jobs. It isn't safe for me to demand that all parties who are accountable act responsibly. I still wind up being the bad guy at family gatherings and in my encounters with officials who should help me attain justice. The pressure is on me to pretend that everything is fine and sacrifice either my integrity or my family.

The other victims that I've met have been my gift from this experience. They affirm my integrity. I feel like a whole person with them. At last I don't feel guilty about making family members uncomfortable. I'm opting on the side of me, regardless of the guilt that others try to lay on me.

My "cellophane wrap" is dissolving into a breathing, healed scar tissue. When I feel strong enough on all levels emotionally, physically, mentally and spiritually, I attempt to attack this problem from a different angle, knowing full well I am opening the wound again. Restoration dictates whether I will live my life out with or without dignity. I'm trying to keep emotion out and good business in during my efforts for restoration.

Recovery comes to me in the form of not feeling bitter or crazy. Perspective tells me that life doesn't offer more to us than a chance to learn and try to make a difference for the better. After I've met with other victims and found myself accepted and understood, there is a sense of joy in human sharing even if it is common pain that we are sharing."

John

"I put an attorney on the witness stand and questioned him today. Most of the time, he hemmed and hawed and answered that he couldn't remember. I know the deck is loaded against me, but it felt good to be on top of my case and able to face an educated thief on my terms. I've lost all respect for the system. Lawyers have cost me everything that I worked a lifetime for. But, I never thought I could do it. I not only did it, it felt good. I guess I keep fighting because I feel responsible to help straighten up this mess before I die. With my last breath, I will fight something that is this wrong.

I know I am recovering because I'm able to read my file and check every document without the pain I used to feel. Even more, I'm able to go into court alone. It used to be so tough to read the documents. I left most of it to my attorney, until I saw what he was doing to me. I sure had a false sense of security with attorneys. I always believed that I could handle my feelings. I never knew emotions were so strong. I wasn't able to eat or sleep after I'd been to court or had to read my legal papers. Now I treat court like a part-time job. When I'm on, I'm on. When I'm off, I rest.

My wife is afraid that this will kill me at my age. I think it would kill me to let it happen and not fight."

Judy is remarried and settled into a comfortable life. She still startles when the phone rings, and has occasional intrusive thoughts and nightmares. She shares:

"I think it is time to reconsider our historical admiration for great conquerors, statesmen and leaders. They must be made to prove their greatness by their deeds. Too often words are just used to divert our attention from the bad guy's deeds. Only responsible and just deeds meet the standard; words must be verified.

My nonexistent husband looked so good. He talked a great story and made a lot of money. I was financially so comfortable. He had friends in high places and soon seemed to have the 'world by the tail.' I judged him by the appearance of a 'diamond in the rough' and was fooled by the trappings of success. I was so proud for responding to this brilliant orphan who needed a home and a fresh start. When I think of his actions versus his words, there were clues. His insistence on getting the mail was a clue. Staying up at night was probably another one. Then I walked into attorneys' traps and believed their words.

I wonder how long I will be cynical. I love my new husband and believe that he is a real person. However, I insist on separate bank accounts.

I would define recovery as cope-ability, if there is such a word. After being a recluse, I feel like I can live in the world again. If a problem comes down the road, I am confident that I can cope. Pain is not frightful anymore.

The attorney who insisted on a $10,000 retainer to take my husband's case in the East finally responded to my request for a refund. He'd done 4 hours worth of work according to my calculations and the brief contact that they'd had. His office informed me that there was no excess to refund. His bill was $2500 per hour, I guess. I don't think I'll take this sitting down. I need to find out what the rules are on attorneys' fees in New Jersey."

Chloe - This lady has won good decisions from judges in court. She has been in and out of court for 15 years, however, and has developed an interesting formula.

> "Any process that takes 15 years for a judge to see the facts and adjudicate according to the law is not only ridiculous but toxic. I have had strong decisions

come my way including the judge forcing my ex-husband to pay me while he appeals paying me.

Regardless, throughout these many years my mind has not permitted me to rest or take comfortable shelter. I have searched for something, anything that would give me sound answers for my plight. Why was I the target of such evil influences? What did I ever do to deserve this? I began to study about cold, calculating personalities who could parade as professionals serving their clients. These are the kinds of people who find the 'cat and mouse' style of court play enjoyable. I ended up studying the sociopathic and psychopathic personalities. I used the information to prepare to meet my opposition in court. It helped. I won more in court and stayed on top of the adversarial situations better.

I long to meet the gentle, the kind, and those without underlying motives. Being seduced by anti-social persons is a horrible experience. They attempted to make a mockery of my life, my values and needs. Their abilities and dark instincts make them the cleverest of the ruling classes on Earth.

My confidence is more hopeful and I'm feeling, at least, in control of my life. The legal system, as it stands today, is no better than any other business that wields power for profit. It is political and does not exist to serve the people.

There must be balanced individual rights against collective rights. Within a family structure, if one child is delinquent, the other children cannot be shunned or disciplined out of assumptions that they may be doing wrong also. The same is true of a society. We must reward those who strive everyday of their lives for a better life and a stronger country."

Recovery and Society

Invisible as they are, specific legal abuses found readily in LAS victims' assaults lance the heart of a healthy society. Justice substantially validates the worth of the citizen and reaffirms his positive social identity. More and more, crime is being recognized as a major health problem. In a climate where it is predicted that every citizen will be a victim of violent or nonviolent crime at some point in his life, the future will be teeming with psycholegal issues. Victims must force and enjoy community resolutions as well as resources for healing. Four attitudes need to be adopted by the community of American citizens.

1. **Oppression and abuse of power are injurious to the health of victims. Domination by abusers of bureaucratic power threatens the very functionality of the public and private sectors in our country (Beguai).**

2. **Victims are not self-interested, narcissistic folks who sit around and wallow in their losses. They are courageous individuals who face their pain and care to right the wrongs. They participate**

in the collision of evil and good as it is classically intended in order to achieve balance. Denial is popular, but far less responsible.

3. Trust is a social staple that must be protected just as earth and water must be protected to provide for survival. When trust is damaged, the community suffers and society as a whole will eventually falter and collapse (Bok). Veterans of crime must exude zero tolerance for lying in courtrooms, lying in political campaigns, lying to cover-up, and deceptions through omittance and nonperformance by public officials and public servants.

4. An oath is a person's word to faithfully serve. USC Title 18 Sec. 1621 states:

> Whoever, having taken an oath before a competent tribunal, officer, or person, in any case in which a law of the United States authorizes an oath to be administered, willfully and contrary to such oath states or subscribes any material matter which he does not believe to be true, is guilty of perjury and shall be fined no more than $2,000.00 or imprisoned not more than five years or both.

Oaths add that touch of personal responsibility that requires a public promise to execute a job according to the law and in good faith. Each case of LAS is a result of a violation of sworn duty. Oaths are usually required to be taken and then are kept on file. They seem to have become a forgotten formality in the course of public service.

LAS pro se victims are digging up violations of these official promises and using them for the matrix of many liens that are being filed against public officials' private properties. Properly done, this is a profoundly empowering act of an average citizen. In the end, trust in a public servant means trusting his word. Those who take oaths must be held accountable. Oaths aren't just a ceremonial frivolity, they are the basis of trust of those in power.

The victim who is betrayed, abused, and torn, and his taker/perpetrator who is unjustly enriched, both must face that there is still nothing valued more by a human being than to be esteemed by himself and his community. Except for the psychopath at the farthest end of the power continuum, the CCs' and PCs' collisions are largely motivated by humanity's deep-rooted need for self and other esteem.

Human beings also need a sense of history and heritage. Addressing psychological and legal issues in the same work may seem like mixing apples and oranges. However, the nucleus of the human being lies within his social systems and his interactions with governments, courts, and bureaucracies that have executive powers. Americans share a unique heritage which stirs the stewing pot of mixed cultures, all of whom are promised a basic right to pursuit of happiness, right to due process and right to redress. LAS cuts to what victims perceive as a severely broken promise.

When American culture esteems that which brings justice and which protects the environment and its citizens, then behaviors will be motivated accordingly. We need to teach the difference between political power, which takes and coerces, versus spiritual power, which inspires and protects. America seems to have lost a national definition of the values and components of a life that is truly good in the eyes of LAS victims.

A breakdown of trust seems to be serving as a rationale for abuse. Insurance companies complain that there is so much consumer fraud that they must fight the payment of all claims with a vengeance. State industrial insurance systems speak of the many malingerers that they must endure. Bankruptcy Court blames fraudulent debtors for their actions and lack of sensitivity. Courts easily use the term "frivolous" to avoid hearing cases. Limited budget and large workloads provide the reasons for nonperformance on the parts of bureaucrats.

As frustration accumulates, the malingerer and the fraudulent debtor, who are PC's in the midst of their scams, are experiencing merely a challenge of their schemes. LAS veterans must see to it that it is no longer adequate to say to a fine, upstanding citizen, "You must endure and understand this pain that we put you through because there are so many scams run on us, so much fraud." If the victim is not a fraud, then it is critical he not be treated as a fraud. If a public servant has a responsibility, he must execute it regardless of workload. These societal changes are in the hands of LAS veterans.

The stories of John, James, Judy, P.J., Chloe and Tom dramatize that equal opportunity under the law and use of courts to achieve justice are foremost in providing conditions that foster the basic rights and the mental and physical health of American citizens. Violations of victims' rights followed by massive system failures are totally preventable causes of emotional injury. Healthy veterans of psycholegal trauma are the richest resource to rely upon for systems reform.

Conclusion

> *The Indians taught their children that people are born with sharply pointed crosses within their chests. When they did wrong, the cross would spin about causing prickly pain. However, if they continued to do wrong, the cross would eventually dull and the pain would no longer be there to guide them toward goodness.*
> (Goodenough)

The President's Task Force in 1982 issued a significant and compassionate report on the plight of victims:

> "The important proposals contained here will not be clear unless you first confront the human reality of victimization. Few are willing to do so. Unless you are, however, you will not be able to understand. During our hearings we were told by one eloquent witness, 'it is hard not to turn away from victims. Their pain is discomforting; their anger is sometimes embarrassing; their mutilations are upsetting.' Victims are vital reminders of our own vulnerability. But one cannot turn away.

> You must know what it is like to have your life wrenched and broken, to realize that you will never really be the same. Then you must experience what it means to survive, only to be blamed and used and ignored by those you thought were there to help you. Only when you are willing to confront all these things will you understand what victimization means."

After twenty years of treating victims, who do I admire? The prosaic and conscience-centered people who comprise the majority of American people are my heroes. Victims who trusted me with their deep selves showed me the inner workings of the ordinary person. What a fine work it is. It comes in the package of the small businessperson, largely the mid classes who have no advocates or financial clout, and those who desire upward mobility, but who won't sacrifice staple values for feigned esteem. They are ambitious and heroic Americans who are invisible houses of American character.

Veterans of LAS, through use of the eight steps, extract the value from suffering. Problems are embraced on the recovery road. Reality becomes the veteran's traveling companion. Mental health is dedication to reality at all costs. With every mile, symptoms of LAS gradually fade. Recovery alludes to no destination. The victim, now grown to veteran, moves forward, greatly relieved and lifted toward hope again. This veteran of LAS will once again look toward the future and feel hungry for growth. Pride in survivorship unfolds and blooms.

I owe my optimism to my LAS patients. They deserve to be affirmed and respected as veterans who can lead the future back to American character as a source of national pride.

K.P.H

Conclusion

Epilogue

7:45 P.M. Wednesday evening.

There were about 60 people in attendance.

The room was well lit. I could easily see the various features of the faces looking at me from the audience who'd come to hear a lecture on LAS.

I paused after about forty five minutes of presentation.

"Are there any questions?"

My eyes scanned the room finally noting an old man raising up in the back row to my right.

A shaky voice broke the moment of silence. This man said:

"I'm at the end of the line."

"You tell me to come to a seminar. You say I can be healed."

He almost shouted, "B.S!"

"I don't have time to take a seminar. I'm broke. I don't have the strength."

All eyes were on this quivering individual who looked to be about 75 or 80 years old. He had dark hair and penetrating eyes. It was obvious that he had not formulated a question but needed to speak. All attention became riveted on him.

I moved away from the lectern inviting him to tell us more.

"A man like me's got to take the law into his hands.

There is no hope when you get like me."

I asked what "like me" was.

"Old, broke, sick and damned mad!"

He shared bits of a story that ended with an attorney taking his old car away from him to satisfy a fraudulent judgement. The rather small, aged man swore that he had proof of everything he said.

"My house burned down," he sobbed.

The audience began to interact with him. I had the sense that if I'd interrupted him, I would have been lynched.

"Didn't you have insurance?" asked one member of the group.

I mentally noted the tone of the question because I would use it later when I addressed "what not to say to a victim." It sounded to my ears like, "Didn't you have insurance, stupid?"

He answered that he did and that the insurance company refused to pay because they accused him of "burn for profit." His sobs heaved at this statement.

"My wife died there, I wanted to die there. I wouldn't burn my house down."

The audience commented sympathetically as the old man sank into his chair and the lecture resumed.

8:32 P.M.

"You can only function within your realm of empowerment," I stated in a effort to bring perspective to the empowerment section of the lecture.

The old man rose up with his fist in the air.

"Here is my realm of power!" he snarled at me. His index finger demonstrated a move that was clearly the pulling of a trigger.

"I am dying. I had a heart attack. Now, I have cancer too.

I told you I don't have time.

Social security wasn't enough to help me with the lawyers. My lawyer took every dime and didn't show up for the final decision.

I got a job at my age delivering bread in my car. Can you believe it? The insurance lawyer took my god damned car and told my boss he would garnishee my wages."

"Here's my power!" showing us his trigger finger again.

"I'll fix the bastards. What can they do to me?"

He stormed out of the room and down the hall. I motioned a colleague to go after him. He was gone into the darkness.

7:00 A.M. Thursday morning. Looking at the morning paper, I worry that I will read about the old man at the lecture.

I wonder if he owns a gun.

Epilogue

Bibliography

Abrahamsen, David. *Crime and the Human Mind.* New York: Columbia University Press, 1944.

Atwater, Lee. "Apologies for Campaign Tactics." U.S. News and World Report. Vol. 110, p. 16 Jan 28, 1991.

Axelrod, Robert. *The Evolution of Cooperation.* New York: Basic Books, Inc., 1984.

Balus, Mary E. "Services for Victims of Crimes: A Developing Opportunity." *Evaluation and Change* Special Issue (1980): 148.

Bard, Morton, and Dawn Sangrey. *The Crime Victim's Book.* New York: Brunner/Mazel, Inc., 1986.

Becker, Howard S. *Outsiders: Studies in the Sociology of Deviance.* New York: Free Press, 1963.

Bequai, August. *White-Collar Crime: A 20th Century Crisis*. Lexington: Lexington Books, 1978.

Berne, Eric. *Games People Play*. New York: Grove Press, 1964.

Bodenhamer, Gregory. *Back In Control*. New York: Simon & Schuster, 1992.

Bok, Sissela. *Lying Moral Choice in Public and Private Life*. New York: Pantheon Books, 1978.

Bos, Candace, and Sharon Vaughn. *Strategies for Teaching Students with Learning and Behavior Problems*. Boston: Allyn & Bacon, Inc., 1988.

Bradshaw, John. *On The Family: A Revolutionary Way of Self Discovery*. Pompano Beach, FL: Health Communications, 1988.

Burger, Warren E. *Significant Supreme Court Opinions of Chief Justice Warren E. Burger*. Manila: Philippine Bar Asso., 1984.

Butcher, Jake. "Financial Crime: Jail for the Fallen Banker." *Time* 17 June 1985: 76.

Calkins, Diane. "Setting Bullies Straight." *Kiwanis Magazine* Feb. 1989: 20-23.

Cole, Diane. "The Entrepreneurial Self." *Psychology Today* June 1989:61-66.

Dershowitz, Alan M. *The Best Defense*. New York: Vintage Books, 1983.

Elias, Robert. *Victims of the System*. New Brunswick: Transaction Books, 1983.

Erikson, Erik H. *Childhood and Society*. 2nd ed. New York: W. W. Norton and Co., 1963.

Financial Management Asso. *Why S. O. B.'s Succeed and Nice Guys Fail in a Small Business.* Phoenix, AZ: Financial Management, 1976.

Flanigan, Beverly. *Forgiving the Unforgivable*. New York: MacMillan Pub. Co., 1992.

Gannon, Patrick J. *Soul Survivors*. New York: Prentice Hall Press, 1989.

Garofalo, James. "Introduction to the National Crime Survey-Analytic Report." *National Criminal Justice and Statistician*. Washington D.C.: U. S. National Criminal Justice and Statistician Service, 1977.

—, and M. J. Hindelang. "An Introduction to the National Crime Survey." *Analytic Report*. SD-VAD-4. Washington, D. C.: Government Printing Office, 1978.

Goldstein, Gerald and Michael Hersen. *Handbook of Psychological Assessment.* New York: Pergamon Press, 1984.

Goleman, Daniel. "Key to Post Traumatic Stress Lies in Brain Chemistry, Scientist Find." *New York Times.* 12 June 1990.

Gottfredson, Gary D. and Denise C. Gottfredson. "Victimization in Schools." *Contemporary Sociology* 16 (1987).

Greider, William. *Who Will Tell the People.* New York: Simon & Schuster, 1992.

James, Edwin, et. al. "Ethics—In and Out of the Classroom." *Time* 16 Feb. 1989.

James, Jennifer. "Out of Control." *Alcoholism and Addiction.* Nov.-Dec. 1986.

Keen, Sam. *Fire in the Belly.* New York: Bantam Books, 1991.

Kiplinger. "Kiplinger Washington Letter", Vol. 64, No. 35.

Koepp, Stephen. "Fraud, Fraud, Fraud: The White Collar Crime Wave." *Time* 15 Aug. 1988.

Kropatkin, Philip, and Richard P. Kusserow. *Management Principles for Asset Protection; Understanding the Criminal Equation.* New York: Ronald Press, 1986.

Kusic, Jane Y. *White-Collar Crime 101.* Vienna, VA: White Collar Crime 101, 1989.

Levine, Harvey R., William M. Shernoff, and Guy O. Kornblum. *Bad Faith Litigation.* Encino, CA: Rutter Group, 1985.

Loehr, James E. *Mental Toughness Training for Sports.* Lexington, MA: The Stephen Greene Press, 1982.

Margenau, Eric A. *The Encyclopedic Handbook of Private Practice.* New York: Gardner Press, Inc., 1990.

Marston, David W. *Malice Aforethought.* New York: William Morrow & Co., 1990.

Mishne, Judith. *Clinical Work with Children.* New York: Free Press, 1983.

McQuade, Molly. *The Wellness Encyclopedia: The Comprehensive Resource for Safeguarding Health and Preventing Illness.* Publishers Weekly: Vol. 237, 1990.

Neiderbach, Shelley. *Invisible Wounds: Crime Victims Speak.* New York: Haworth Press, 1986.

O'Connor, Nancy. *Letting Go With Love: The Grieving Process.* Arizona: LaMariposa Press, 1984.

Parsonage, William H. *Perspectives on Victimology.* Beverly Hills: Sage, 1979.

Pines, Ayala, Elliot Aronson, and Ditsa Kafry. *Burnout: From Tedium to Personal Growth.* New York: The Free Press, 1981.

Popcorn, Faith. *The Popcorn Report.* New York: Doubleday Dell Publishing Group, 1991.

Rappaport, J. *Community Psychology: Values, Research and Action.* New York: Holt Rinehart and Winston, 1977.

Reasoner, Robert. "What Is the Source of Self-Esteem." *Self-Esteem Newsletter* 5.1 (1989):

Reese, James, James Horn, and Christine Dunning. *Critical Incidents in Policing.* Washington, D.C.: U. S. Department of Justice, 1991.

Reiff, Robert. *The Invisible Victim.* New York: Basic Books, Inc., 1979.

Ringer, Robert J. *Looking Out for Number 1.* Beverly Hills: Los Angeles Book Corp., 1977.

Roskies, Ethel. *Stress Management for the Healthy Type A.* New York: Guilford Press, 1987.

Schafer, Stephen. *The Political Criminal.* New York: The Free Press, 1974.

—, *Compensation and Restitution to Victims of Crime.* Montclair, N.J.: Patterson and Smith, 1970.

Selye, Hans. *The Stress of Life*. New York: McGraw-Hill, Inc., 1956.

Shaver, K. G. *Introduction to Attribution Processe and The Attribution of Blame, Causality, Responsibility and Blameworthiness*. New York: Springer Verlag, 1985.

Shellow, Jill. *Grantseekers Guide: A Directory for Social and Economic Justice Project*. Chicago: National Network of Grantmakers and the Interreligious Foundation for Community Organization, 1980.

Slaby, Andrew E. *Aftershock*. New York: Fairoaks Press/Villard Books, 1989.

Stein, Sol. *A Feast for Lawyers*. New York: M. Evans and Co., 1989.

Stewart, James Brewer. *The Constitution, the Law, and Freedom of Expression 1787-1987*. Carbondale, IL: Southern Illinois University Press, 1987.

Stich, Rodney. *The Real Unfriendly Skies*. Reno, NV: Diablo Western Press, Inc., 1990.

Tucker, William. *Vigilante*. New York: Stein and Day, 1985.

Ullman, John, and Steve Honeyman. *The Reporter's Handbook - An Investigator's Guide to Documents and Techniques*. New York: St. Martins Press, 1983.

Williams, Janet B., ed. *Diagnostic and Statistical Manual of Mental Disorders.* Rev. 3rd ed. Washington D. C.: American Psychiatric Asso., 1988.

Wilson, James Q., and Richard Herrnstein. *Crime and Human Nature.* New York: Simon and Schuster, 1985.

Woititz, J. G. *Adult Children of Alcoholics: Common Characteristics.* Hollywood, FL: Health Communications, 1983.

Zegan, L. S. *HandBook of Stress, Theoretical and Clinical Aspects.* Ed. Goldberger and Breznitz. New York: Free Press, 1982.

Glossary

adjudication—the judicial decision that ends a criminal proceeding by a judgment of acquittal, conviction, or dismissal of the case.

affidavit—a written statement which the writer swears is true.

alleged—said to be true, but not yet proven to be true; until the trial is over, the crime may be called "the alleged crime," for example.

appeal—a request by either the defense or the prosecution that the results of a decision on certain motions or of a completed trial be reviewed by a higher court.

arraignment—the appearance in a court of an accused person at which the court may inform the accused of the charges against him or her, advise the accused of his or her rights, appoint a lawyer for the accused, and/or hear the plea of the accused. The meaning of arraignment varies widely among jurisdictions.

assault—an illegal and intentional physical attack or attempted or threatened attack by one person against another. Assaults are commonly divided in the law into aggravated assault, which is generally a physical attack in which serious bodily injury is inflicted or there is a threat or attempt to inflict serious bodily injury with a deadly weapon, and simple assault, in which a threat, attempt, or actual attack is made without serious bodily injury or the use of a deadly weapon.

attorney—a person trained in law and authorized to advise, represent, and act for others in legal proceedings. An attorney may also be called a lawyer, a counsel, or an advocate.

beyond a reasonable doubt—the degree of proof needed for a jury or judge to convict an accused person of a crime.

charge—an allegation that a specific person has committed a specific crime; the filing of the charging document may be called "pressing charges."

civil court—a court that hears cases concerned with the alleged violation of civil law; not a criminal court.

civil law—the law relating to private, not criminal, matters in which one party sues another for remedy.

complainant—the person who makes a formal criminal complaint; also, the victim of the crime described in the complaint.

complaint—a formal written statement made by any person, often a prosecutor of a victim, and filed in court to accuse a specific person of committing a specific crime.

continuance—a delay or postponement of a court hearing; the case is said to be "continued" when it has been delayed or postponed.

corroborating witness—a person who is able to give information that supports the statements made by either the victim or the accused.

court—an agency of the judicial branch of the government authorized by statute or constitution to decide controversies of law and disputed matters of fact brought before it.

defendant—a person who has been formally charged with committing a crime.

defense attorney—the lawyer who represents the defendant in a legal proceeding. Victims are generally not required to talk to the defense attorney except in court.

disposition—the final judicial decision which ends a criminal proceeding by a judgment of acquittal or dismissal, or which states the sentence if the accused is convicted.

double jeopardy—putting a person on trial more than once for the same offense. Double jeopardy is forbidden by the United States Constitution.

evidence—testimony and objects used to prove the statements made by the victim and the accused.

eye witness—person who saw the crime take place.

grand-jury hearing—a legal process in which citizens selected by law and sworn to investigate criminal activity and the conduct of public officials and to hear the evidence against accused persons sit as a jury to decide if there is enough evidence to bring the accused to trial; unlike court trials, grand jury hearings are generally closed to the public and their proceedings, by law, are secret.

hearing—a legal proceeding in which arguments, witnesses, and/or evidence are heard by a judicial officer or an administrative body.

information—a formal written accusation, made by a prosecutor and filed in a court, alleging that a specific person has committed a specific crime.

initial appearance—the first appearance of the accused in the court which has jurisdiction over his or her case; the appearance may include a formal reading of the charges, the plea and/or the setting of bail, but the accused may merely be informed of his or her rights and asked if he or she has a lawyer. Different jurisdictions have different policies at the first appearance.

investigation—the gathering of evidence by law-enforcement officials and in some cases prosecutors, for presentation to the grand jury or in court, to prove that the accused did commit the crime.

judge—a judicial officer who has been elected or appointed to preside over a court of law.

jury—a group of citizens who are selected by law and sworn to determine certain facts by listening to testimony in order to decide whether the accused is guilty or not. The jury in a trial is called a <u>petit jury.</u>

legal—something based upon, or authorized by law... something in conformity with the positive rules of law; permitted by law; as, a "legal" act.

mirroring—a response by the listener that reflects the same or similar experience on the part of the listener as the victim is sharing.

motion—a verbal or written request, made by the prosecutor of the defense attorney before, during, or after a trial, that the court issue a rule or an order.

notice—a written order to appear in court at a certain time and place.

perjury—deliberate false testimony under oath.

perpetrator—a person who commits a crime.

plea—a defendant's formal answer in court to the charge that he or she has committed a crime.

privileged relationship—a relationship wherein communication is protected by confidentiality.

Appendix A

Clinical Post Traumatic Stress Disorder - Defined

A. The person has experienced an event that is outside the range of usual human experience and that would be markedly distressing to almost anyone, e.g., serious threat to one's life or physical integrity; serious threat or harm to one's children, spouse, or other close relatives and friends; sudden destruction of one's home or community; or seeing another person who has recently been, or is being, seriously injured or killed as the result of an accident or physical violence.

B. The traumatic event is persistently reexperienced in at least one of the following ways:

1. Recurrent and intrusive distressing recollections of the event (in young children, repetitive play in which themes or aspects of the trauma are expressed.)

2. Recurrent distressing dreams of the event.

Clinical Post Traumatic Stress Disorder - Defined

3. Sudden acting or feeling as if the traumatic event were recurring; includes a sense of reliving the experience, illusions, hallucinations, and dissociative (flashback) episodes, even those that occur upon awakening or when intoxicated.

4. Intense psychological distress at exposure to events that symbolize or resemble an aspect of the traumatic event, including anniversaries of the trauma.

C. Persistent avoidance of stimuli associated with the trauma or numbing of general responsiveness (not present before the trauma), as indicated by at least three of the following:

1. Efforts to avoid thoughts or feelings associated with the trauma.

2. Efforts to avoid activities or situations that arouse recollections of the trauma.

3. Inability to recall an important aspect of the trauma (psychogenic amnesia).

4. Markedly diminished interest in significant activities (in young children, loss of recently acquired developmental skills such as toilet training or language skills).

5. Feeling of detachment or estrangement from others.

6. Restricted range of affect, (e.g., unable to have loving feelings).

7. Sense of a foreshortened future, e.g., does not expect to have a career, marriage, or children, or a long life.

D. Persistent symptoms of increased arousal (not present before the trauma), as indicated by at least two of the following:

1. Difficulty falling or staying asleep.
2. Irritability or outbursts of anger.
3. Difficulty concentrating.
4. Hypervigilance.
5. Exaggerated startle response.
6. Physiologic reactivity upon exposure to events that symbolize or resemble an aspect of the traumatic event (e.g., a woman who was raped in an elevator breaks out in a sweat when entering any elevator).

E. Duration of the disturbance (symptoms in B, C, and D) of at least once month.

(American Psychiatric Association, 1987, pp.250-251)

A-4

Appendix B

Resources for the Empowerment of the Ordinary Person

Resources for Victims are seen as a starting place. The writer or publisher is attempting to help link-up victims with helping organizations. No guarantees are made as to results from contact with the following organizations or is responsibility accepted for the outcome of any alliances established from this list.

>American Institute of Stress
>124 Park Ave.
>Yonkers, NY 10703
>(914) 963-1200
>
>Studies the effects of stress on health.
>
>Americans for Legal Reform
>35 Pinelawn Road
>Suite LL8
>Melville, NY 11747
>(516) 420-1212

Focused on New York and reform for family court as well as reform in general

Antishyster Newspaper
PO 540786
Dallas, TX 75354-0786
(800)477-0786

Tells of court experiences of victims including research and creative legal information

C.A.L.L. (Citizens Against Legal Loopholes)
12730 Carmel Country Road, #120
San Diego, CA 92130

A citizens group dedicated to exposing fraud and corruption in the U.S. Bankruptcy system.

Consumers for Legal Reform
P.O. Box 4754
Irvine, CA 92716-4754
(714) 854-0881

A citizens group dedicated to legal reform of the civil justice system.

Fully Informed Jury Association
P.O. Box 59
Helmville, MT 59843
(406) 793-5550

Urges changes in law to empower juries to be instructed to judge both the law and the facts in a case

HALT - Americans for Legal Reform
1319 F St. NW, Suite 300
Washington, DC 20004
(202) 347-9600

A group of attorneys who organized to stop "legal tyranny."

Institute for Victims of Trauma
6801 Market Square Dr.
McLean, VA 22101
(703) 847-8456

Committed to respond effectively and quickly to increasing incidence of stress disorders from victimization.

International Society for
Traumatic Stress Studies
435 Michigan Ave. Suite 1717
Chicago, IL 60611
(312) 644-0828

Conducts research and treatment on persons who experience severe mental or emotional reactions to extraordinary stressful situations.

Legal Research Foundation
PO Box 1794
Bristol, CT 06011-1794

Dedicated to helping those without attorneys to find the most pertinent legal research for their cases and the prior cases that have been successful.

National Association for Crime Victims Rights
PO box 16161
Portland, OR 97216-0161
(503) 252-9012

"Fed up" with increase in crime and excessive violence. Works to reverse overconcern with criminals' rights.

National Association of Crime Victim Compensation Boards
PO Box 16003
Alexandria, VA 22302
(703) 370-2996

Develop better methods of administering existing programs to enhance public awareness of programs for crime victims and form liaisons between victim advocacy groups.

National Organization for Victim Assistance
1757 Park Road NW
Washington, DC 20010
(202) 232-6682

Works for decency, compassion, and justice for all victims. Works for legal change and advocacy.

National Victim Center
107 West 7th St. Suite. 1001
Fort Worth, TX 76102
(817) 877-3355

Seeks redress for injustices done to victims. Promotes public awareness, judicial responsiveness and prevention.

NOLO Press
950 Parker Street
Berkeley, CA 94710
(510) 549-1976

Publishes self-help law books and software

Resources for the Empowerment of Ordinary People

VICTRE - Victims of Invisible Crimes
Treatment, Restoration, and Education
P.O. Box 28917
Las Vegas, NV 89102
(702) 593-9925

Helps victims of nonviolent crimes and deceptions to network for support and legal empowerment; currently developing a network on the internet.

White-Collar Crime 101
8300 Boone Boulevard
Suite 500
Vienna, VA 22182
(703) 848-9248

Services geared for prevention and reporting of White-Collar Crimes through education, and a handbook is published.

Excerpt from Tom's petition to the United States Supreme Court seeking to address the most basic Constitutional rights of every citizen of the United States which penetrates the facade of all invisible victims:

A Petition for Writ of Certiorari filed with the United States Supreme Court

Questions presented for review:

1. Does each private individual, protected by the laws of the United States, possess an absolute and inalienable right to redress?

2. Does each private individual, protected by the laws of the United States, possess an absolute and inalienable right to due process of law relating to disputes involving life, involving its liberty, or involving its property, within all proceedings brought under the laws of the United States and/ or the laws of the several individual states?

3. Does a Federal issue arise directly under the first, fifth, seventh, and tenth amendments when one or more federal courts, *sua sponte*, intervene, misstate facts otherwise determined by a jury at a proper trial, and obstruct the execution of a judgment

against a judgment debtor liable under state and common law?

A brief of An *Amicus Curiae*, U.S.C. Title 36, allows members of the public to support an issue before the court as a friend of the court with knowledge of the facts of the case. There are stringent rules to be followed and the above citation needs to be researched for appropriate use and presentation. However, in Tom's case, several supporters filed *Amicus* briefs in support of his Writ of Certiorari because the fundamental Constitutional issues of life, liberty, property and the pursuit of happiness are raised in Tom's case.

On October, 1993, Tom was informed by the Clerk of the Supreme Court of the United States that he would not be granted Certiorari. This means that the Chief Justices of the Supreme Court of the United States elected not to consider hearing his case. Tom had asked the Court to reaffirm the fundamental Constitutional rights of a citizen of the United States.

The highest court of the land has chosen to sidestep this basic Constitutional issue. Tom and other victims of legal abuse have taken their fight to Congress.

Getting Important Evidence from the Government

One of the tools that is available to you to obtain the information necessary to protect your rights is the Freedom of Information Act which requires government agencies to provide you with information that you request, provided that the information would not jeopardize national security and is not part of the evidence that the government is compiling as part of an active criminal investigation.

Freedom of Information Act Request

The letter on the following page is an outline of a formal Freedom of Information Request which can be used with any local, state or federal government agency. Remember to keep a copy of your letter for your files, and to insure that the agency received it, send your request by Certified Mail, Return Receipt Requested.

If you do not receive a response by the agency within 30 days, follow-up with another letter or telephone inquiry as to the status of your request.

In the event that your request is denied, you can appeal the denial and, if necessary, go to court to get a court order for the information that you requested.

A-14   Resources for the Empowerment of Ordinary People

                                                        Date

Name of Agency Official
Title
Name of Agency
Address
City, State, Zip

Dear_____:

     Under the provisions of the freedom of Information Act, Title 5, U.S.C. § 552, I am requesting access to . . . (_identify the records as clearly and specifically as possible_).

(*The following paragraph is Optional:*)

     I am requesting this information because . . . s̲tate the reason for your request if you think it will assist you in obtaining the information.)

     If there are any fees for searching for, or copying, the records I have requested, please inform me before you fill the request. (O̲r̲:̲ . . . please supply the records without informing me if the fees do not exceed $_____.)

     As you know, the Act permits you to reduce or waive the fees when the release of the information is considered as "primarily benefiting the public." I believe that this request fits the category and I therefore ask that you waive any fees.

     If all or any part of this request is denied, please cite the specific exemption(s) which you think justifies your refusal to release the information and inform me of your agency's administrative appeal procedures available to me under the law.

     I would appreciate your handling this request as quickly as possible, and I look forward to hearing from you within 10 working days, as the law stipulates.

                                    Sincerely,
                                    (Signature)
                                    Name, Address and
                                    Telephone Number

Legal Abuse Syndrome A-15

Date

Name of Agency Official
Title
Name of Agency
Address
City, State, Zip

Dear_____:

    This is to appeal the denial of my request for information pursuant to the Freedom of Information Act, Title 5 U.S.C. §552.

    On *(date)*, I received a letter from *(individual's name)* of your agency denying my request for access to *(description of the information sought)*. I am enclosing a copy of this denial along with a copy of my original request. I trust that upon examination of these communications you will conclude that the information I am seeking should be disclosed.

    As provided for in the Act, I will expect to receive a reply within 20 working days.

(Optional Paragraph:)

    If you decide not to release the requested information, I plan to seek redress of this matter before the appropriate court.

(Optional: It is sometimes helpful to set out some of your legal arguments in your administrative appeal. Otherwise, all that the appeal authority has is the denial authority as argument.)

                              Sincerely,
                              (Signature)
                              Name, Address and
                              Telephone Number
                                        (Ullman)

A-16

Appendix C

Victims-Witness Protection Act of 1982

Title 18 U.S.C. §1515 states:

"Findings and Purposes" "...(2) All too often the victim of a serious crime is forced to suffer physical, psychological or financial hardship first as a result of the criminal act and then as a result of contact with a criminal justice system unresponsive to the real needs of such victim, and "...(#) Although the majority of serious crimes falls under the jurisdiction of State and local law enforcement agencies, the Federal Government, and in particular the Attorney General, has an important leadership role to assume in ensuring that victims of crime, whether at the Federal, State, or local level, are given proper treatment by agencies administering the criminal justice system."

"...the term 'physical force' means physical action against another, and includes confinement;
...the term 'misleading conduct' means-
(A) knowingly making a false statement;

(B) intentionally omitting information from a statement and thereby causing a portion of such statement to be misleading, or intentionally concealing a material fact, and thereby creating a false impression by such statement;

(C) with intent to mislead, knowingly submitting or inviting reliance on a writing or recording that is false, forged, altered, or otherwise lacking in authenticity;

(D) with intent to mislead, knowingly submitting or inviting reliance on a sample, specimen, map, photograph, boundary mark, or other object that is misleading in a material respect; or

(E) knowingly using a trick, scheme, or device with intent to mislead;

    (5) the term 'bodily injury' means-

(A) a cut, abrasion, bruise, burn, or disfigurement

(B) physical pain;

(C) illness;

(D) impairment of the function of a bodily member organ, or <u>mental faculty</u>; or

(E) any other injury to the body, no matter how temporary.

Representative Brooks News Release

November 6, 1991
Washington, D.C. 20515

Brooks requests G.A.O. probe of Justice Department's U.S. Bankruptcy Trustee system

Mismanagement, conflicts of interest, and political cronyism are hindering the effectiveness of the Justice department's U.S. Bankruptcy Trustee Program, witnesses told a House Judiciary Committee panel today. In response to this testimony and numerous complaints he has received, Congressman Jack Brooks (D-Texas) announced that he is requesting the General Accounting Office to conduct a thorough investigation of the program.

"A smoothly functioning bankruptcy system is vital to the well-being of the American economy," said Brooks, Chairman of both the Subcommittee on economic and Commercial Law and the full Judiciary Committee, "and congress created the U.S. Trustee Program to be a cornerstone of that system. Unfortunately, the examples of abuse that have come to our attention provide a clear signal that the U.S. Trustee Program is simply not getting the job.

The U.S. Trustee Program, housed in the department of Justice, performs a wide range of administrative functions in bankruptcy cases, including monitoring cases, holding creditors meetings and reviewing fee requests. For example, in Chapter 7 liquidation cases the U.S. Trustees establish the supervisory panels of private trustees who act as fiduciaries for individual debtors' estates. U.S. Trustees are also intended to serve as the watchdogs of the bankruptcy system to ensure fairness and ferret out fraud and abuse.

"Since 1987," continued Brooks, "17 former trustees and five of their employees have been convicted of embezzling funds in excess of $6.1 million from bankruptcy estates-- and I am afraid this is just the tip of the iceberg. Given the increasing numbers of bankruptcy filings at a time of deep and lingering recession, we cannot afford to take chances with the Trustee Program."

Lawrence A. Beck, a bankruptcy attorney from San Antonio, Texas, criticized the U.S. Trustee System from the debtor's viewpoint. He encountered disorganization and resistance from the local U.S. Trustee when he sought help in investigating gross irregularities in the private trustee's handling of the debtor's estate. "Most individual debtors who enter bankruptcy with significant assets," said Beck, "eventually conclude that they have become trapped in a crooked, dishonest system which is run for the benefit of the panel trustees and his hand-picked attorney, and which is supervised by incompetent bureaucrats."

George Francis Bason, Jr., a former bankruptcy judge, told the Subcommittee that despite a promising start in 1978, the U.S. Trustee Program has suffered "significant deterioration" in recent years. According to Bason, political favoritism and conflicts of interest are among the chief causes of this decline.

"Cronyism has come to have too large a role in appointments in the U.S. Trustee system," said Bason. "Competent people at the local level are leaving in disgust... and too many of the remaining personnel in both the national and the local offices are simply not qualified by background and experience to do their jobs efficiently and well."

With respect to conflicts of interest, Bason told the subcommittee that as a judge he presided over two cases with national and international significance in which he "found that intense pressure was exerted by the national office upon the local office of the U.S. Trustee to abandon the U.S. Trustee's proper independent role as a neutral, impartial administrator and instead to act as a servant and advocate for the narrow self-interest of one party to the litigation."

Larry E. Kelly, Chief Judge of the U.S. Bankruptcy Court for the Western District of Texas, echoed Bason's charges of political favoritism in the Trustee Program. Kelly also testified that the "major defect" in the Trustee Program is "a lack of devotion and purpose in its very existence from the uppermost levels of the Justice Department. I have, with recent exceptions... seen no indication that the program has any pride or discernible purpose in its leadership."

Brooks concluded: "I, for one, am not going to stand by while those caught up in the crippling economic crisis facing this country are subjected to further abuse by those entrusted with the fair administration of the bankruptcy system. I am determined to see that the U.S. Trustee Program gets back on track."

A-22 **Beyond Rage *and Back* Worksheets**

Appendix D

Beyond Rage... *and Back* Worksheets

The processing sheet helps to pinpoint the injuries and the injurers. Until we claim the injury and therapeutically blame the injurer, we cannot balance the scales and let go. Prioritized offenders will emerge as the processing occurs. Sometimes this will have an element of surprise a sense of control begins to return when we know the "who and what."

Identify possible hostage-takers. These can be agencies, individuals or various systems.

Who assaulted you first?

Who has stolen from you?

Who is responsible for your losses?

Who are you angriest at?

Who has used misinformation against you?

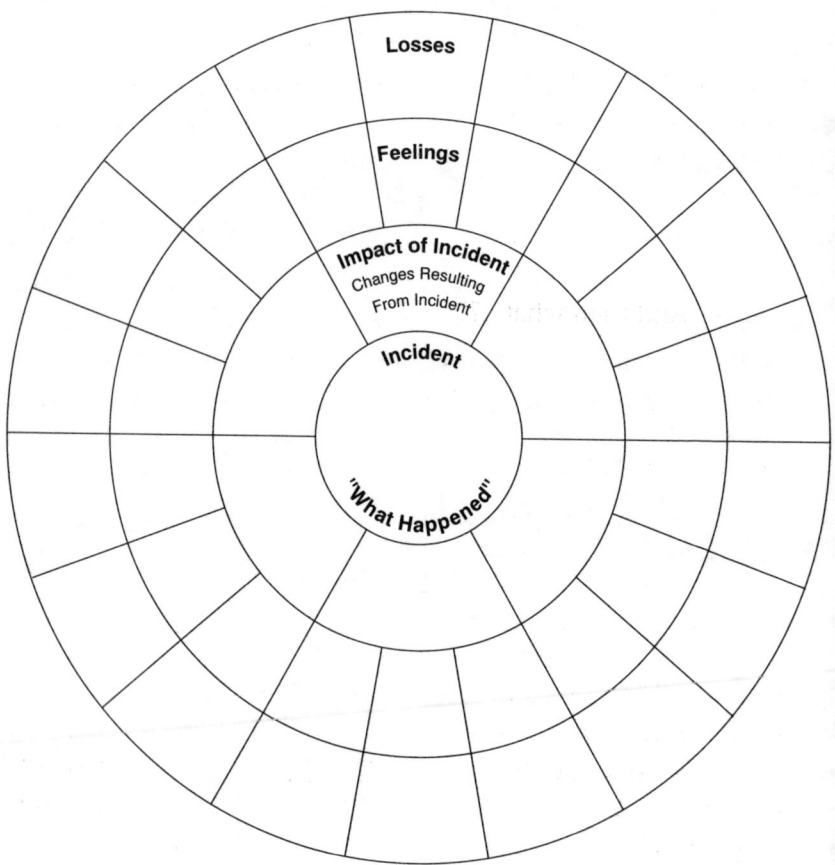

The Feelings and Symptoms Circle

Next, as the sender, write feelings and emotional experiences in the designated circle. Include symptoms, all physical, mental and emotional symptoms. Use the list of feeling words and the following lead-ins to help pinpoint the emotion(s) expressed. Remember, you are not expected to clinically diagnose PTSD or LAS. The cognitive and emotional aspects of debriefing are not designed to ascertain or rule out a clinical diagnosis of post trauma stress.

Ask and answer again and again in terms of emotional reactions:

1. "And then what...?"

2. "And then how were you feeling?"

The listener helps to expand on the feelings by reflecting:

1. "Sounds like..."

2. "You felt as if..."

3. "From your point of view or perception..."

4. "It felt as if..."

5. "It seemed as if life..."

If you are alone, you can ask yourself or volunteer to share with your listener:

1. "At that point I just felt like…"

2. "The whole world seemed…"

3. "I felt like I needed,.."

4. "In my deepest heart I felt…"

5. "My sleep became…"

Other:

The Loss Circle

The next step is to identify losses in detail. These will include material and nonmaterial losses. Take time to consider losses to society as a whole. Victims are very sensitive as to the expansive nature of their experiences. Society's losses are sorely felt by responsible victims.

Write your losses in the circle.

1. First fill the circle with material losses:

    property

    money

    personal treasures regardless of monetary value

2. Now, move on to nonmaterial losses:

    List at least 3 beliefs, and more if you can, that represent losses from your former belief system.

    1. "What did I believe before the event(s)?"

    2. "What do I believe now?"

    3. "What is happening as a result of the experience?"

4. "What should be happening?"

Considering the philosophical and spiritual side of your losses, ponder and discuss these questions:

"Why me?"

"Who has been affected?"

"How do you explain the crime or assault, if you can?"

"Do you relate it to past "bad" behavior?"

"Do you blame yourself?"

"How deep does the damage go?"

"To what am I vulnerable?"

"What can I not control?"

"What feelings have changed?"

"What moral law was violated?"

"Do you feel abandoned by God?"

"What losses to society as a whole exist from this experience?"

Legal Abuse Syndrome A-29

Did your victimization reach the point of post traumatic stress disorder?

PTSD Subscale for Invisible Victims

Answer True or False:

1. ____ I have a good appetite.
2. ____ I wake up fresh and rested most mornings.
3. ____ My daily life is full of things that keep me interested.
4. ____ Once in a while I think of things too bad to talk about.
5. ____ I am sure I get a raw deal from life.
6. ____ At times I have fits of laughing and/or crying that I can't control.
7. ____ No one seems to understand me.
8. ____ I have nightmares every few nights.
9. ____ I find it hard to keep my mind on a task or job.
10. ____ I have had very peculiar and strange experiences.
11. ____ At times I feel like smashing things.
12. ____ Most anytime I would rather sit and daydream than do anything else.
13. ____ My sleep is fitful and disturbed.
14. ____ I am a good mixer.
15. ____ I have not lived the right kind of life.
16. ____ I wish I could be as happy as others seem to be.
17. ____ I am troubled by discomfort in the pit of my stomach every few days or more often.
18. ____ Most of the time I feel blue.

19. ____ I usually feel that life is worthwhile.
20. ____ I regret things more often than others seem to.
21. ____ At times I have a strong urge to do something harmful or shocking.
22. ____ I don't seem to care what happens to me.
23. ____ Much of the time I feel as if I have done something wrong or evil.
24. ____ I am happy most of the time.
25. ____ Often I feel as if there were a tight band about my head.
26. ____ I believe that my home life is as pleasant as that of most people I know.
27. ____ Sometimes I feel as if I would like to injure either myself or others.
28. ____ I lose out on things because I don't make my mind up fast enough.
29. ____ Most nights I go to sleep without thoughts or ideas bothering me.
30. ____ I have had periods in which I carried on activities without knowing later what I had been doing.
31. ____ I am afraid of losing my mind.
32. ____ I frequently find myself worrying about something.
33. ____ I dream frequently about things that are best kept to myself.
34. ____ I am never happier than when alone.
35. ____ I am so touchy on some subjects that I can't talk about them.
36. ____ Once in a while I think about things too bad to talk about.

37. ____ I have had peculiar and strange experiences.
38. ____ I easily become impatient with people.
39. ____ I have certainly more than my share of things to worry about.
40. ____ If I were dead, it would be okay.
41. ____ Most of the time I wish I were dead.
42. ____ I have strange and peculiar thoughts.
43. ____ I hear strange things when I'm alone.
44. ____ Terrible words come into my mind and I cannot get rid of them.
45. ____ Sometimes some unimportant thought will run through my mind and bother me for days.
46. ____ Even when I'm with people I feel lonely much of the time.
47. ____ I have sometimes felt that difficulties were piling up so high that I could not overcome them.
48. ____ It makes me feel like a failure when I hear of the success of someone I know.
49. ____ Whenever possible I avoid being in a crowd.
50. ____ I don't have the energy to start a new project.

Scoring:

Count the number of False answers for questions 1, 2, 3, 14, 19, 24, 26, and 29.

Place the total here_____

Now count the number of True answers for questions not listed above.

Place the total here_____

Add the totals together and rate degree of interference with a satisfying life:

Manageable discomfort	1 - 8
Life feels distasteful	9 - 17
Interference is of concern	18 - 27
Serious PTSD, needs therapeutic assistance	28 - 50

With slight modification, this test is adapted from Keane, T.M., P.F. Malloy and J.A. Fairbank). Empirical development of an MMPI subscale for the assessment of combat-related post-traumatic stress disorder. <u>Journal of Consulting and Clinical Psychology</u>, <u>52</u>, 888-891.

A-33

Index

Absolutely What Not To Say To A Victim 42-46
Abuse of power 5, 8, 12, 96, 132, 156, 207, 210
Alfred Adask 7, 148
American Psychiatric Association 166
Barriers to blame 87
Belief system 31, 39,122
Beyond Rage 13
Blaming actions 97, 99, 100, 102, 120
Blame styles . . . . 89 - 92
Brain hormones 21, 22
"Cellophane wrap" 2, 20
Center circle 34
Compartmentalization 80,81,196
Conscience vs Power 107,115
Conscience-centered 108, 112, 113, 114, 116, 117,
                   118, 120, 121, 125, 127, 130, 132, 175
Constitutional rights 150, 188, 200
Cooperation 109, 110, 115, 120, 121

Credibility	129, 164
Debriefing	30, 32, 35, 41, 49, 125
Deceptive crimes	4
Down-aging	146
Envy	116, 119, 126
Equation for white-collar crime	187
Fact circle	35, 36
Forgiveness	194
Freedom of Information Act	173
Fritz Heider	96
Golden Age of the Victim	84
Guilt	85, 86, 88
Guilt and shame	108
Hans Selye	29
Hints for helpers	40, 42
Hostage	2, 5, 8, 142
Becker, Howard	85
Invisible crimes	1, 4
LAS reframe checklist	132
Loss circle	27, 38
Loss of status	63, 65
Mediation and arbitration	100
Menninger	84
Mental toughness	181, 182
Myths to be dispelled	117
Oath	208
Obsessive styles	69-74
Oppression	156, 157, 197, 207

Positive sum	115
Post Traumatic Stress Disorder	19, 21, 23, 24, 30, 109
Power-centered	108, 111-113, 115, 116, 118, 120-122, 126, 130
President's Task Force, 1982	213
Pro Se	156, 173
Punishment	96, 101
Rapid Response	159
Recovery	193, 197, 207
Reframing exercise	134 - 139
Restoration	195, 196
Revenge	93, 94
Self-Blame Checklist	90
Selye, Hans	29
Skills for empowerment	154
Suicide	26
Symptoms of Hostage Stage	2
Takings	57, 60, 61
Tit for Tat	111, 113 128
Trust	208, 210
Vigilante	40, 185, 186
Violations of moral code	98
Walking wounded	31
Zero sum	115, 116